D0943282

HEALING STORIES
OF GRIEF AND FAITH

From Denial and Despair
to Comfort and Peace

Kathrine Palmer Peterson

Garrison Oaks Publishing
44 Lords Lane
South Berwick, ME 03908

1-888-349-5220

Published by:
Garrison Oaks Publishing
44 Lords Lane
South Berwick, Maine 03908

Publisher's Cataloging-in-Publication Data

Peterson, Kathrine Palmer.
  Healing stories of grief and faith : from
 denial and despair to comfort and peace /
Kathrine Palmer Peterson. [et al.]--1st ed.
    p. cm.
    Includes index.
    LCCN: 2002094720
    ISBN: 0-9666405-9-4
1. Death 2. Inspiration 3. Bereavement
4. Adjustment 5. Spiritual

I. Title

BF575.D35 2003   155.9'37

Dedication

This book took approximately four years to write and compile but is based on a lifetime of learning and loss. It is dedicated to my mother, Fannie Roach Palmer a woman of faith, strength, and courage who has been an incredible inspiration in my life.

To my husband, Richard Peterson, an unbelievable soulmate, thank you for your encouragement and love.

To my brother, Steve Palmer, the most compassionate person I have ever met, thanks for always being there when I've needed you.

This book is also dedicated to the memory of my father, Edward G. Palmer, Jr. and all those precious souls who have gone on before us.

Acknowledgments

To the many contributors of this book who gave so much of themselves, thank you for sharing a portion of your lives that is so intensely private. Through you and your generosity we are able to learn more about grief and ourselves.

Thanks to Cindy M. Denault, an exceptional editor, who has a keen eye for errors.

Scripture quotations are from the New International Version of the Bible. Copyright © 1985 by The Zondervan Corporation.

Other helpful grief resources are: *Write from Your Heart, A Healing Grief Journal* and *After the Tears, A Gentle Guide to Help Children Understand Death.* This journal and video have been recognized as valuable teaching tools by counselors, teachers, and parents.

Order info at: 1-888-349-5220

Warning - Disclaimer

Table of Contents

1. INTIMATE STORIES OF LOSS

2. GROW IN STRENGTH

Contents

5. PET TALES OF LOVE

Contents

6. RAINBOWS AND BUTTERFLIES

7. COMFORT AND PEACE

Contents

8. BONUS CHAPTER -
WRITE FROM YOUR HEART

Introduction

To heal, according to Webster's Dictionary, is to restore to health. Therefore, if you are healing you are working toward health. A person suffering from grief is dealing with a wound just as real and potentially harmful as any physical wound. There are no magic potions or operations that will cure a broken heart and because the symptoms of grief aren't always visible, it is possible that others are unaware that you are suffering emotionally, and possibly, with a spirit that is deeply crushed.

Often times I hear from grieving individuals who believed that life only contained the mental and physical realm. They assumed that if they took care of their mind and body they would achieve a balance in their life. Of course they didn't find peace until they realized that the human body also has a soul, a spiritual need that was waiting to be discovered and nurtured. When these individuals opened their minds, hearts, and souls to God great things occurred.

The purpose of the information and the heartfelt stories in this book is to help you achieve a greater degree of well being. As you read this book search for comfort and peace through faith and through the wisdom that is shared from individuals who have mourned and gained insights that only the bereaved have knowledge of.

God bless you all at whatever stage of grief you may be experiencing. **May you receive personal healing and great comfort as you reflect on** *Healing Stories of Grief and Faith.*

Preface

If you are reading this book it is likely that you have lost someone very dear to you or know someone who has. The stories in this book will touch anyone who has ever lost a loved one no matter what the circumstances might have been. The individuals that share their lives with us are people who have opened the most secret places in their hearts to tell us of their fears, emotions and thoughts on the subject of grief. Who better to describe how it feels to lose a loved one than those who have experienced the devastating loss and pain personally? Who could better tell us about the war but the soldiers who were in the battle? In this instance, the soldiers are those who have managed to get through their grief to once again find productivity, love, comfort, hope, and even joy in their lives.

As you travel on your own grief pilgrimage may you find the journey a bit easier after you read the stories from individuals who have navigated a similar course before you. They will share their personal questions, doubts, and concerns and then reveal what they discovered along the way. May you find peace and comfort in God's great love.

Chapter One

Intimate Stories of Loss

No matter what our loss or circumstance, we are all alike in that the loss of a loved one changes our lives dramatically. The dreams and plans you had hoped for are altered. You are forced to make the journey through grief and suddenly find yourself left to cope with the reality that your future no longer includes the one you loved so dearly. You may be full of questions, doubts, anxiety, and emotions that you are unaccustomed to and don't understand; you may be shaken and anxious for God's direction. What do you do now you ask?

God has given you the emotion of grief as a healthy means of coping. It is normal and natural to cry and grieve. Showing your emotions in public does not indicate that you aren't a good Christian. You may even feel pressured to think that you are expected to handle grief with the stoicism of a martyr.

The truth is, the Bible tells us in John 11:34 that Jesus wept. How powerful that verse is. It is comforting to know our Savior knows how we feel. God has designated a time to grieve. Ecclesiastes 3:4 tells us there is a time to weep and a time to laugh, a time to mourn and a time to dance.

It is clear that the grieving process is necessary even for Christians. However, the nature of the grief of a Christian who has placed faith and trust in the work that Jesus did on the cross is different than it is for the unbeliever. We believe that death is not an end to life but the beginning of our eternal life with Christ. Paul said it well in Philippians 1:21 when he stated: "For to me, to live is Christ and to die is gain."

As believers it is comforting to know that we will see our loved ones in Heaven where there is no pain or suffering. We have loved and lost people whom we cherished — it is normal to miss their physical presence in our present life and to yearn for their fellowship in our future.

There is great expectancy for Christians as we look forward to the day we are reunited with Christ and our loved ones. We can take comfort in God's promise when Jesus said, "Blessed are those who mourn, for they will be comforted" (Matthew 5:4). God knows our pain and suffering and has promised us a Comforter, the Holy Spirit. He will give us peace even in the midst of grief.

God has given us tears as a method for the body to cleanse itself. Tears of joy and tears of pain are not the same tears. Tears are cleansing for the system and have been magnificently created as part of our complex and often misunderstood system. Just as the body has incredible ways to heal a wound to the skin, it also has been extraordinarily created to mend wounds of the heart. Tears and grief are a part of that amazing process. Allow yourself to go through the natural grief process that will assist in the healing of your emotional wounds.

William Cowper, an English hymn writer said, "Grief is itself medicine."

Grief is the most intense emotion you will ever encounter because it is so passionately mixed with love. How you react to your emotions and your situation will determine how well you survive the ordeal, and will determine the path your life will take from this moment on.

When someone you love dies, your life is irrevocably altered forever—and whether you have lost a child, spouse, parent, sibling, relative, or friend grieving must take place for healing to begin.

It has been said that time will heal your feeling of loss—this is misleading—time never healed anything; only God can heal and does so in time. A common theme you will read from many of the contributors is that you never get over a death, you learn to live with it. God can give you the comfort and peace you need to face your loss.

If you are wondering how you are going to make it through one day, let alone the rest of your life, then read on. Listen to the stories of people who have cried in anguish and survived.

These pages are filled with experiences of caring individuals who selflessly shared their insightful thoughts and heartfelt emotions to help us understand the true process of grieving.

Sharing and Caring for One Another

As you read the following stories, that come deep from the heart, imagine that you are here with us, among friends. Sit back in your chair, take a deep breath and relax. We ask you to join us at our gathering where we are all sitting face to face and are able to reach across the table and comfort one another. My friend, Donna Bradley, has invited you to be with us at her imaginary tea party and expresses her invitation this way. "In my mind's eye I imagine that we are all sitting in a beautiful garden somewhere, talking over tea poured out of Bone China teapots. There are delicious scones with Devonshire cream and berry spreads and fresh sandwiches on tables that are covered in beautiful linens with lace. There are vases of freshly cut flowers in our midst, the perfume permeates our surroundings like the angels among us all.

The sun is bright and warm and the ocean breeze touches our skin as we laugh and cry and talk about all we have accomplished, individually and as a group—we discuss the intimate details of our grief that only the bereft understand. I smile every time I see my old friends stopping by in numbers that are gradually increasing at our tables!"

Please come join us as we come together in fellowship and describe the pain, love, trials, and triumphs that have become a part of our lives. Learn how others have found peace and comfort through it all—discover how you, too, can find solace and contentment.

We begin with a story from Linda, a compassionate widow from Brooklyn.

"All that I once knew, everything that I defined myself with, disappeared!"

"Joel and I were married almost thirty years and he has been gone thirteen months.

I had just turned fifty when he died. I asked myself, "Is that all there is?" Thirty years of marriage and now in thirteen months, I'm starting to get those questions about dating from the well meaning, but uninformed crowd. If I take care of myself, and if God so decrees, I could be around until I'm eighty. I keep asking myself what is it that I am supposed to do for the next thirty years? I can't keep tagging along after my son and his girlfriend. Soon, they will get married and have their own home and family.

I just can not picture myself as the widow with the cat, babysitting the grandchildren all the time. I certainly look forward to the grandkids someday in the future, but I am so terrified of being one of those lonely, little old ladies who has to live with her children and helps out by caring for the grandchildren. I've been teaching for more than twenty years, and the day will come in the not too distant future when I will have to retire. Frankly, I totally dread that. There are times I am so lonely, I wish I could work seven days a week just to have other people around me. I have found that it is best not to dwell too long on the prospects for the future, or wonder if there will be a future for me.

It is going to be a long time before I begin to think of myself as I once was. When Joel died, I lost so much, not only my husband, lover and best friend, but my identity, my friends, my social life, my conception of myself and my life. All that I once knew, everything that I defined myself with, disappeared. I have been told that it is common for a widower or widow to lose their identity and self esteem with the death of a spouse.

All my roles in life changed—I have not yet begun to redefine my life or myself. In fact, I do not have the foggiest idea where to begin. I know I used to have a life and I keep going back to the shelf where I know I left it; but it is not on that shelf, and try as I might, I cannot find it anywhere.

For almost thirty years, I knew who I was and what my roles were. Now, I no longer know. "Linda" was always defined as part of Joel and the roles I had in life were built out of that relationship. Those roles no longer exist, and therefore, my image of myself no longer exists either. Linda as I knew her, and Linda as I was comfortable, just isn't here any more. I am concentrating on taking life "one day at a time."

Our second story comes from Stephanie, a young widow. She nervously began her story and focused her eyes on the table in front of her, reluctant to look at anyone. Then she slowly looked around at the sympathetic faces and somehow got the courage to speak the words that described her pain.

"It helps me cope if I only let in a little grief at a time and focus on getting through one day– today."

"When others ask me how long it takes to heal and what is normal behavior, I can only tell them what I experienced. It is different for each one of us. The first few weeks, the pain is intense and the realization that a loved one has died is still a foreign feeling that takes time to accept. My advice is not to make great demands on yourself concerning how fast you should heal. Healing can take years, not months like many would have us believe.

At first I could not eat, read, sleep or make decisions properly—I could not think. At around two to three weeks I began to emerge from the worst of the shock (not from the grief, just from the initial shock.) Then my head and emotions began to clear a little each day. I began to rest a little better and I called people whom I knew cared about me. I was able to garden a little bit and I knew this activity was giving my body and my grief-stricken soul a rest.

I am surviving by only letting in a little grief at a time, and by focusing on just getting through one day—today. Sometimes I go hour by hour because I find it too exhausting and overwhelming to think too far ahead or to look back.

I have found that I must cry and I have learned not to hold the tears in. I used to cry every night when I was alone in bed, when I missed my husband not being there next to me. Each day, mentally, I count the days he has been gone. Today it will be seventy-seven days—I miss him."

Next to share with us is Bethany, of New Hampshire, a well-dressed businesswoman with dark hair that she wears in a tight bun.

"I am healing as time passes, I have to."

"I have not had the luxury of taking much time off from work because I have to support the children and myself. We were struggling financially before my husband passed away and now I feel a great burden. I am tired all the time and many times I feel overwhelmed with life and responsibilities. It has not been a full year yet and I am beginning to feel as though I will survive. I know the journey will be a long, hard one that I can not fully fathom. I do know that it is getting easier with time.

I have discovered that some days I can function without crying at every turn or mention of his name. One day I was surprised when I realized that I had gone a whole week without crying. This healing in itself was unsettling—I felt guilty. Whenever I enjoy life I feel a pang of unfaithfulness. How can I laugh with him gone?

I may appear happy on the outside but inside I ache and I know this is normal. I will take any moment that gives me a brief reprieve from my grief. I have a life that needs to be lived to the fullest. I have children who need their mother to give their lives direction.

Other widow friends object to my use of the word "heal". They claim that grief is not a disease that can be cured. I totally agree with them to that degree of the general definition, but how else can we describe the process of recovery—of accepting the loss and finding fulfillment in life again? I will always mourn the loss of my husband and never "get over" the loss, but I am healing as time passes, I have to."

LaTanya, a petite woman with dark hair and cobalt eyes shares her story next. She nervously grasps her grief journal as she relates her story.

"My life is in His hands"

"Jackson's accident happened in Maine. He was driving home on a slippery winter night when another driver ran a red light and crashed into him. I lost everything that day. Jackson was the perfect man for me. When he wasn't working he enjoyed being with me. We enjoyed hikes with my nephews at a local park and being with family and friends. When he was home we always enjoyed being together even if we were just working around the house. He loved to build and whenever he had a project he asked me to go outside with him—just for the company. I even went on the roof with him when he shingled and worked on the chimney. One day he carried a 90 pound bag of shingles and a small sun chair to the top of our two story roof so that I could sit in a chair while he worked; he placed the chair in a valley where I would be safe.

We enjoyed each other's company every moment we were together; life was perfect. He was always so thoughtful and made me laugh dozens of times every day. We would talk while he worked and I always found him fascinating. Those memories may seem silly, but they were precious to us. We didn't have to do something special or go somewhere exotic to have fun. Being together was enough, no matter what we were doing. I praise God for the memories I have and the precious moments that we had together. I remember them with an ache in my heart, but I am fortunate to have had those moments to remember.

At first it was painful to discuss all of the particulars of the accident, but now it is, in an odd way, healing for me. Whether people are just curious or ask because they sincerely care, it doesn't matter. It helps me to talk about Jackson and how much I loved him.

At first I was in total shock and denial. I could not understand how God could let this horrible accident happen.

In my mind, I had planned how my whole life would play out and Jackson was the leading star in my dreams. How could I possibly face the rest of my life without him? I was shocked and lonely; but God taught me a lesson in love. He showed me the magnitude of his great love for me, and he showed me that I am not the one who writes my life's story. Surely I can plan, hope, and dream, but my life is in His hands. I don't know what the future holds for me right now and that requires me to lean on Him more. I am willing to see where I am led and what life holds for my future. I know how precious time is. I know God loves me with a love that is greater than any other. When I remember my darkest moments of sadness, despair, and agonizing pain, I realize how God has taken my weaknesses and transformed them into an inner strength. Not that this strength will replace Jackson, but it will help me live my life purposefully. God is faithful and His word is true. I am learning to lean on Him more and more every day. On the days when I find it hard to pray I simply pray, "Please help me God" and I know that He hears my prayer and I am comforted knowing He is always with me."

We welcome Steve, a grieving father, who is the next to share his story; it is one of great tribulation and sorrow. He tells us of the valuable lessons he learned as he came to a new knowledge and understanding of life.

"I decided that it was time to put Bill's death behind me and go forward with my life."

"My son died just before Christmas, and the holidays have not been the same since. My daughter was eight months pregnant at the time with her first child, who was born on January 8th. I was so consumed by my grief that I was unaware of what was going on in my life.

My boss called on the third day of my leave of absence from work (we were allowed three days for immediate family members) to let me know what my schedule was. I explained to him that I was not ready to go back to work yet. He gave me a few more days to grieve and then he called and gave me an ultimatum; either I come back to work or lose my job.

I told him what he could do with his precious job. I was not ready to deal with people. A child is not supposed to pre-decease its parent, your mind is conditioned that your parents will predecease you (not that that loss is easy, because it is not.) Many questions went through my mind—like: "Why does God take a young life right in the middle of his prime?" I remember one instance—the very next Christmas—I went to the store to buy a gift for my granddaughter. I was walking through the toy department and the tears were flowing down my cheeks. One of the sales ladies asked if she could help me find something. Then she commented that it was Christmas, and that I shouldn't be crying. It is a time for joy and happiness—I struck out at her with hatred. "You try losing a child at Christmas and see if you don't cry." I said this in a moment of sheer pain and I have felt remorse for the pain I caused that poor unsuspecting lady.

I got divorced that year after being married for nineteen years. My father died the next year. It took me many months before I even recognized that we had an addition to the family (my first granddaughter.) I isolated myself for six months after Bill died. I did not leave my apartment for anything.

My network of friends and family brought food in, my pastor and others came in to chat with me frequently, and many times, I could not even deal with them—I cried at almost anything. Later during that six-month period, I did start getting out a little. I was running low on money, paying the rent and bills wiped out my savings—I needed to get back to work. I found I still could not deal too well with people, and went from job to job. I finally landed the job I have now and have been promoted several times over the past five years.

I was at my new job for only two months when I started having some aches and pains in my chest—I thought it was my lungs (I was an ex-smoker, and I had regularly associated with smokers.)

Then on December 7th my heart stopped. What I really mean to say is that my heart stopped beating. I was as close to death as you ever want to be without actually having been pronounced dead.

Fortunately, there were people around and I was revived fairly quickly, rushed to the hospital and had an angioplasty. Dec. 7th was an important day because Bill died on Dec. 7th, two years to the day of my heart attack.

The angioplasty did not help for too long, a few months later my heart stopped again. Once again I was near other people and was in the hospital quickly. This time, they took me into emergency surgery and replaced four of my major arteries around my heart. The operation was supposed to have lasted about seven hours, but nine hours into the operation, my family started asking questions as to why it was taking so long. The head surgeon came out to talk to the family and answer questions and so forth. With a sense of urgency, he asked the family if I had a pastor available because they thought that last rites were in order.

My mother told the doctor that I had said that I wouldn't be coming out of the operation. This alarmed the doctor enough that he went back in and worked on me for a couple more hours. After over eleven hours on the table, they wheeled me out into post-op. My family and a preacher kept vigil for the next couple of days while I lay there in a coma.

I had apparently given up and had willed myself to die. Waking up out of the coma was the hardest ordeal of my life—nightmares—but when I did open my eyes, I found my whole family there including my daughter and my oldest granddaughter (yes, she had another daughter during this period.)

They were all so happy to see me. Even the nursing staff was cheering. My thoughts on death had immediately changed and I knew that I had returned because of God.

After a few hours of thinking about some of the events and people who had come into my life, I decided that it was time to put Bill's death behind me and go forward with my life.

My strength returned very quickly. Within three days, I walked up and down three flights of stairs at the hospital, and within four days after waking up, I was released from the hospital. Two weeks later (three weeks from the day of surgery) I went back to work. Now, let me qualify why my heart failed in the first place. I have no history of heart disease in my family. I no longer smoked—I had quit about fourteen years before this incident.

I did not have high blood pressure, and I did not have high cholesterol. I led a moderately active lifestyle. The stress of losing Bill was the most important factor in this case, and the medical doctors did not want to believe that. They wanted to believe that there was some medical reason for my heart problems. Since then, the doctors have come to the realization that stress was a mitigating factor in my case.

I have been well since—I have come to terms with Bill's death. I can talk about it, but the grief is still there and it probably always will be. Even though years have passed, certain instances can and do trigger a tear from time to time.

This has been my story. God has played a strong part in my life—I have experienced miracles and I believe that this is one of them. I believe that God has walked beside me during several trials. I found it important to give my troubles over to a Supreme Being. Do not let grief stay bottled up inside of you like I did, talk about it!

Death, as we all know, is a part of life. We read about it in the papers, we hear about it on the news. We might even offer various sundry forms of condolences to people who are grieving. Yet, as a result of our exposure to this part of life—we have become somewhat conditioned to it happening to the "other" person. Almost complacent, until it (death) comes knocking on our door.

Then the table turns. We wonder why others do not feel our pain. Many of our friends and acquaintances shun us because they themselves don't know what to say or do not know how to deal with our pain.

Sometimes I feel as though I want to shout, "Can't you see I am hurting?" "I have lost my son—where has everyone gone?" Our best friends and those who have experienced this pain stay, because they can feel our pain."

The following realizations came to me because I lived through my loss and the experiences afterward:

1. God would have carried much of the burden for me, all I had to do was to open up my arms and accept him and let him in.

2. Bill would not want me to die as a result of his death.

3. It is important to talk with people. Talk to living people!

4. God is alive!

Know that you are not alone and that part of the healing is to talk to others. You can't keep grief of this magnitude to yourself. If you do, it will surely eat you up inside and will not let you go. I was lucky, despite my sometimes lack of faith, God stood by my side. They say that God works in mysterious ways—that He has a plan for all of us—if my story of survival can comfort others, then maybe I am fulfilling His plan for me.

Lisa is next to speak, her story is different from the others, because her son, Brooks, lived through a horrendous accident. However, her insight into dealing with trauma and lost friendships is worth special inclusion in this section.

**"My son taught me that attitude is everything. I learned that it is okay to say goodbye to the ones who can't or don't want
to be a part of your life. Life will not only go on, it will go forward and blossom like spring. When things change you must also change to survive."**

Lisa Sitko, CIC, LUTCF

"My youngest child, Brooks, had been in a horrific car accident and was taken to the hospital with massive head trauma. He had been a passenger in a vehicle when it was hit head on.

I arrived at the scene a few minutes after the accident to find my son lying beside the road, grievously injured. He was airlifted by helicopter to a hospital and listed in critical condition. There I remember lying on the cold bathroom floor of the hospital.

Nothing made sense. I couldn't decide whether rage or fear consumed me more. My stomach ached and my knees hurt. There was no comfort in wrapping my arms around myself. I couldn't imagine relief. Everything had changed. Life as I knew it was over—completely over.

I heard the nurses and doctors whispering about my son. Their voices droned on and on but I couldn't understand what they were saying. Brain injury? I kept hearing that. I just wanted to know if he would be able to see again. I wanted to know if he was going to want to live, but he couldn't talk to me. He talked to me at the accident, when he was lying on the ground with his face crushed. He said, "I love you, Mom. Thank you for everything."

Then the helicopter took him away from me, forcing me to go home, get out of my pajamas into some clothes, and drive 45 minutes to the hospital.

It felt like my heart had been ripped out of my chest. My head was pounding. My inner self was saying, "don't have a stroke now—keep it together—it isn't over."

Despair, hopelessness, anger, rage, and fear filled my soul. I needed to get up off the floor. God, help me please. God, are you still there? I can't feel you in my heart. God, I can't live if my child dies. Please, please, God, don't let this be real. Let it be a nightmare and let me wake up, God, from this pain.

Then I knew what I was feeling—it was fear— the most powerful, all consuming, controlling emotion I have ever felt. There was something else now; he spoke, and I felt a fleeting glimmer of hope. Did I dare hope? "God, give me strength. I need more strength than I have ever needed for anything. Please, God." I prayed.

Today is two years after my son's accident. When I allow myself to recall the incident, I relive all of the emotions as if it happened yesterday. It hasn't turned out like I thought it might. People I was sure would be there weren't. It was disappointing but not devastating. The good news is that people I didn't think care, did care.

The world is filled with angels; they found my son and I and more than made up for the disappointments. My marriage dissolved. My friends, some of them new, stepped in and helped at every level. The angels are still here.

I have had so much time to think since this accident. I realize now that I never let anyone help me; I am more comfortable giving than taking. I have learned it is important to let people help. It is also justifiable to say goodbye to the ones that can't or don't want to be a part of your life. Life will not only go on, it will go forward and blossom like spring. You will grow with these changes, just as I did. I fought these changes, but they were stronger than I was. I couldn't stop them. My life changed without my permission. I am able to see that the changes have been for the better. My life is improved, more full, complete now. The fear has subsided; the sadness has diminished. It is true that although I may never get completely over what I saw, my faith is keeping me strong.

If you are struggling like I did to even force yourself to get up, take a shower, or eat, then you are exactly where I was two years ago. Pray about it. Ask for strength. Don't ever blame yourself or anyone else.

Forgiveness allows your soul to cleanse itself. You owe yourself or anyone who disappoints you when you need them, a little forgiveness—Why?—because it is better for you. It will help you heal. Allow yourself to enjoy today. Allow yourself to feel good again. Allow yourself to look forward to tomorrow.

Tragedy can change your direction, but with God's help you will keep climbing the mountain, one step at a time, until you reach the top. My son who was so seriously injured tells me attitude is everything. He is living his life. He isn't afraid of his life.

"God, help me to have the same faith in you my son does, please help me catch up to where he is in his thinking."

May God and your angels watch over you in your journey. Close your eyes and feel their closeness. Let them help you with your grief; it can't be altered, slowed, dulled, or eliminated. Allow yourself to know your feelings instead of postponing or stifling them. If you suppress them, they will resurface at a most inconvenient time. Pray. Talk to God. If tragedy can't be stopped, He will still listen and answer your prayers. Don't give up. Never quit. Pray. Remember to forgive, especially yourself.

I was blessed that my son did survive, but it never occurred to me that he would be so different. The child he was had somehow been drastically changed. I look for answers and am going through the grief process as a result of realizing he is not, and will never be, the same person.

I cannot describe the absolute shock that goes along with recovery in a closed head injury. I also know that to some who have lost people through death that I must sound incredibly ungrateful and selfish.

I really am not, I'm just adjusting to the new situation. When things change you must also change to survive. I am ecstatic over Brooks' progress and his strength and spirit; he has encouraged me as he never gives up; he still never complains although I know he has a lot of back, neck and shoulder injuries that aren't completely resolved. He never felt sorry for himself. I did— plenty.

I also experienced horrible post-traumatic shock from this and realized that if I saw an accident I had to stop until I could determine that none of my family was involved. I don't do that anymore, but I must have looked like a complete nut while I was doing it. I also made contact with a crisis intervention group through the sheriff's department here. It's a group of volunteers who donate twenty hours a month or so to go to accident scenes and assist the injured and/or survivors. They only have training twice a year and I will be going to the next one.

One thing that would have really helped me tremendously while we were at the hospital would have been talking with someone who had been through a similar situation who could have given us hope. The hospital staff wasn't even cautiously optimistic. They only prepared me for the worst, and they didn't know or think about a positive outcome.

I want to volunteer to assist families who are going through this, because I have been through it and we survived. I know one of the reasons our situation was more successful is that Brooks was never alone. He was only in a coma during the lifeflight to the hospital, other than that he was awake and talking or listening to us when it was too painful to talk.

No hospital has enough staff to do that; families need to be there and be involved. God must have a very special purpose for this wonderful man. I am so proud to be his Mom."

Hope in Him

The losses and trials of this life
May surely cause despair.
But faith is kindled in our hearts,
Because our Lord is there.
He carries our burdens and our fears
When we are apt to doubt.
So lean on him and you will learn,
What love is all about.

Kathrine Palmer Peterson

Chapter Two

Grow in Strength

During our lives each of us will face times of joy and sorrow, strength and weakness, love and loss, good times and bad times. Be prepared for the inevitable problems that you will encounter. Learn how to draw on your faith through the spectrum of emotions and experiences that will inevitably come your way.

The following collection of outstanding stories were chosen to uplift your spirit and give you strength through faith.

Jump Into Jesus' Arms

Tony Evans

"Lord, save me!" --Matthew 14:30
Read It: Matthew 14:28-31

Let me give you another important truth you need to know about your trials: Christ loves you even as He tests you.

When Peter stepped out on the water, he started out great, because he started out by faith. It took a lot of faith to step out of that boat. But he got in trouble when he took his eyes off Jesus and started looking at his circumstances. Now this was the same storm Peter had already been watching for about twelve hours. But it looked different out there on that dark water. He let what he saw around him control him. His faith faltered.

The moment Peter took his eyes off Christ, the trial started swallowing him up. If your trials are swallowing you up, it's because you are looking at the wrong thing. You are looking at your trials. I know you can't just close your eyes and ignore them, but they are not to be your focus.

Well, at least Peter had the good sense to cry out to Jesus for help as he was going under. He went to the right place, because Jesus loved Peter far too much to let him go under. Notice there was no delay in Jesus' response. He grabbed Peter "immediately" (v. 31). Even if you are going under, Jesus loves you enough not to let you sink.

In fact, I believe that one major purpose of trials is to teach us that we can't make it ourselves and that we can't figure it out, and all we can do is pray, "Lord, save me!" His love says yes to that admission of need and dependence upon Him.

Of all the temptations you need to resist in times of trial, the greatest is the temptation to think Jesus must not love you very much, or this wouldn't be happening to you.

Recently, my granddaughter, Kariss, got scared by our dog Casey. He ran toward her, and she screamed and came running to me yelling, "Poppy, Poppy! Casey is going to get me!" Then she jumped up into my arms—and from up there, everything looked different. She wasn't afraid anymore.

Has your trial got you scared? Jump up into Jesus' arms. From up there, your trial won't look so fierce anymore. It may still bark, but you're in Jesus' arms now!"

Nevertheless We Must Run Aground

Elisabeth Elliot

Have you ever put heart and soul into something, prayed over it, worked at it with a good heart because you believed it to be what God wanted, and finally seen it "run aground"?

The story of Paul's voyage as a prisoner across the Adriatic Sea tells how an angel stood beside him and told him not to be afraid (in spite of winds of hurricane force), for God would spare his life and the lives of all with him on board ship. Paul cheered his guards and fellow passengers with that word, but added, "Nevertheless, we must run aground on some island" (Acts 27:26).

It would seem that the God who promises to spare all hands might have "done the job right," saved the ship as well, and spared them the ignominy of having to make it to land on the flotsam and jetsam that was left. The fact is He did not, nor does He always spare us.

Heaven is not here, it's There. If we were given all we wanted here, our hearts would settle for this world rather than the next. God is forever luring us up and away from this one, wooing us to Himself and His still invisible Kingdom, where we will certainly find what we so keenly long for.

"Running aground," then, is not the end of the world. But it helps to make the world a bit less appealing. It may even be God's answer to "Lead us not into temptation"—the temptation complacently to settle for visible things.

His Still Small Voice

"From Faith to Faith" by Kenneth and Gloria Copeland

Have you ever noticed that you are sometimes aware of certain things even before you know what the Word says about them? **That's because the Holy Spirit is inside you, teaching you the truth. He speaks into your spirit. Then your spirit relays His promptings to your mind.** Suddenly, you'll have a new thought. "I need to forgive that person," you'll think, or "I need to stop saying those unkind things."

As you become more aware of the Spirit of God in your everyday affairs, you'll be quicker to hear and obey those promptings. You'll actually get in the habit of allowing the Spirit of Truth to reveal the will of God to you. And, believe me, that's one habit God wants you to have!

One of the first things that the Spirit said to me when I began to listen to His promptings was "spend more time in prayer." As I obeyed, I began to be impressed to spend at least one hour a day in prayer.

After I'd begun to do that, He revealed it to me in His Word (Matt. 26:40).

Since then, I have talked with people from all over the world who are hearing the same thing. Believers everywhere are hearing the Spirit of God direct them to more prayer.

God hasn't given the Holy Spirit to just a few special Christians. He's given Him to all of us. And if we'll just learn to be sensitive to His voice, He'll guide us into all truth!

Think about how different your life would be if you knew the truth of God about every situation! Doesn't that just make you want to listen to your spirit? Doesn't it make you want to be on the keen edge of what God is saying?

Start tuning your ear to His still small voice within you. Honor Him and welcome His guidance into your every day affairs. Listen for His promptings and be quick to obey. He's ready to speak to you.

"But the anointing which ye have received of [God] abideth in you, and ye need not that any man teach you: but as the same anointing teacheth you of all things, and is truth." (1 John 2:27)

Overcoming Turbulence

Kathrine Palmer Peterson

I was flying solo in a Cessna-150 in the most turbulent air I had ever flown in. Even strapped in my seat I was bouncing inside the cockpit like popcorn in a popper. My seatbelt consisted of a series of straps that included shoulder bands that secured me tightly to the seat; this safety measure prevented me from being flung away from the controls or into the cockpit ceiling.

At the time of this flight I was a fledgling student pilot. Thankfully, my determined flight instructor, Jean Hardy, had persistently tested my knowledge and skill on emergency procedures.

She knew one wrong move or a distraction could prove fatal. We practiced every possible scenario until my reactions had become instinctive. Today, I would be thankful for every minute of my training.

It was obvious that my present situation with the severe weather made it imperative that I return to my base airport. I cautiously began a 180-degree turn but was tossed so violently that I was unable to continue. I was shaken more as I hit a new pocket and sunk with such speed that it forced me sharply against the restrictive straps, knocking the breath out of me. I was riding the winds like a bucking bronco. The situation was becoming increasingly perilous, I took a deep breath as I gathered my courage, and quickly glancing at the instruments on the panel before me I began my turn. The second attempt was as frightening as the first. I again battled against the power of nature, but I had confidence that God was with me and that I would be able to make it on the third endeavor.

With both hands tightly on the yolk and every muscle tensed—I tentatively eased the yolk to the left, entering the turn and holding it steady until the maneuver was completed.

Success was finally mine—at least so far—I was headed home. Still bouncing and jostling inside the old plane, I fought the wind and the excessive turbulence with such effort, that beads of sweat formed over my upper lip.

At last Littlebrook Airpark was in sight. I surveyed the runway a mere 50 feet by 2500 feet, an adequate airfield but small by general standards. A quick glance at the orange windsock confirmed what I already knew; it was blowing as hard as a trumpet at reveille.

I moved my attention to another factor worth consideration, a natural cliff that lay just beyond the end of the runway. This drop off had proven fatal to four individuals during a takeoff after they experienced mechanical problems. I didn't want to become another statistic. Landing at Littlebrook on a good day was challenge enough, but on a windy day the difficulty factor increased 10 fold—I knew this would be my most difficult landing yet.

Jean's previous lessons and cautionary advice rolled over and over in my mind, "On a windy day come in high and fast not low and slow," she always instructed.

"Apply rudder to keep the plane on a straight path, this prevents the plane from being blown off course." I mentally reviewed all the warnings I could remember.

As I approached the final leg of the landing pattern, I concentrated on each procedure that needed to be carried out. I had practiced these landings countless times before and began to automatically execute each step with precision.

The little red and white plane responded to the demands placed on it. I was now in the landing pattern at the proper altitude, lined up parallel to the runway. A quick radio call to the airport to notify anyone in the area of my location was next on my agenda. It is customary to begin and end the radio call with the name of the airport. Other information that must be included are stating the aircraft numbers that are boldly painted on the side of the airplane, and noting the position held in the landing pattern. Lastly, I would give the identifying numbers that indicated which end of the runway I would land on. Pressing a button on the yolk to activate the radio, I clearly spoke into the receiver that was attached to my headset. "Littlebrook Airport this is 7 November Quebec downwind for three zero, Littlebrook."

I took one hand off the yolk to make adjustments to the controls—I added carburetor heat, then I reduced the power to 1700 RPMs and added 10 degrees of flaps.

While I made a gradual 90-degree turn onto base, I again made the required radio call. "Littlebrook this is 7 November Quebec on base for three zero, Littlebrook." I dropped the flaps to 20 degrees and continued to drop altitude, I was now at 700 ft. and dropping. I made the final radio call and rolled the trim wheel.

Approaching the runway I considered that I might have to abort the landing if I couldn't keep the plane lined up properly or hold it on course. A decision to land or abort the landing must be made within seconds to complete a safe go around. The go around procedure once started requires fulfilling certain steps in rapid order. I mentally went through each step. 1. Full throttle 2. Carburetor cold, push the lever in 3. Flaps— retract them a notch at a time. 4. Set trim for the normal climb.

Thankfully, I wouldn't need to go around this time, I was lined up perfectly for a straight shot landing. Due to the heavy winds I would have to slip it in.

A slip is a maneuver that consists of pressing on the rudder to aim the plane into the wind to keep from blowing off course.

The plane actually glides down to the runway with the nose of the plane angled away from the intended landing area, at the last moment the rudder is released and the plane faces directly toward the targeted landing area long enough to touch down. On this final stretch my arms worked the yolk as I fought to control the plane, my foot pressed on the left rudder as I attempted to keep the plane steady—never before had I experienced a landing this intense.

I worked the controls every second of the descent and hit the centerline on the runway. The back wheels made a thudding squeal and then after a bounce, the plane floated down smoothly onto the nose wheel. I thanked God as I heaved a tremendous sigh of relief and rejoiced that I had landed safely.

This incident reminded me of a favorite saying of seasoned pilots, I chuckled to myself as I recalled the words, "Every landing you can walk away from is a good landing. Every landing you can walk away from and reuse the plane is an awesome landing."

I realized with clarity that my bumper sticker had it backwards. It reads, God is my co-pilot. There is a second sticker that has it right, it states, If God is your Co-pilot then you're in the wrong seat!

Being a pilot in the New England area has many benefits. The beautiful majestic White Mountains are glorious to view any time of the year. The coastal view stretches endlessly for those who crave the ocean panorama. To have the opportunity to experience these breathtaking scenes a person will once in a while encounter dark times of storms and turbulence such as the one I had encountered. The same can be said of life, there will be glorious mountains and valleys to experience.

As I reflected over the events of the day I realized that just as I had been prepared for the many emergencies I would face in the sky, I also needed to be prepared for turbulence in my own daily life.

As a pilot I learned to fly by studying hard and practicing, honing my abilities until the moves I made were instinctive. It was a great revelation when I realized that if I practiced my spiritual emergency procedures as well as I did my flying maneuvers; I would be better prepared for any situation life would send my way.

There will be trouble—turbulence—in our life whether we are ready for it or not.

Life isn't always easy, loss is never easy, but there is hope for you to find peace, comfort, and guidance through His word.

Prepare yourself to handle the trials in your life by honing your spiritual knowledge until you can operate instinctively with faith and confidence.

Be prepared for unexpected turbulence. As you read these four simple spiritual rules, may God open your mind and spirit to his teachings.

The Four Golden Rules for Spiritual Emergencies.

1. Seek God for His guidance and wisdom.
2. Pray and remain strong in your faith.
3. Read the Bible so that you may grow in faith and be comforted.
4. Grow in peace and knowledge through reading and praying and then reach out to others.

I have Survived on the Prayers and Encouragement of Friends and Family.

Shirley Caviness

Yesterday was a year since our angel went home to be with the Lord, and the days leading up to it were very hard. I have survived on the prayers and encouragement of friends and family. God is good all the time even when we can't feel his presence. Sometimes he treats us like his children and has us go as far as we can before he catches us. Most of the time, we think we can't go any further but he knows we can take another step.

This reminds me of the time I was teaching my oldest grandson how to swim, he didn't want me to let go of him and backup, but I knew he could make it six more inches even when he didn't. If I had never let him try it on his own, he would not be the wonderful swimmer that he is now. He would have continued to rely on me to catch him and not have grown strong.

My prayer is that I continue to grow stronger. I want to be a better person because I had the blessing of having known Justyn.

How You Can be Victorious Over Worry

Kathrine Peterson

My childhood was joyous and held few worries for me because my parents carried the burdens— I was one of their children and, of course, they wanted what was best for me. Because I trusted them I sought their wisdom and guidance. As I grew older, even though I was a Christian, I developed a habit of worrying. By allowing this inclination to continue I robbed myself of God's peace. My pitiful attempts to "fix" problems myself instead of relying on God and His infinite wisdom always caused inner turmoil.

My lack of faith to totally trust in Him changed one day as I prayed for answers to this problem— the words and music to a song that I thought had been long forgotten came to mind. O what peace we often forfeit, O what needless pain we bear, All because we do not carry, Everything to God in prayer.

This was a song that I remembered my parents singing in church—they knew the words by heart and didn't need to read from the hymnal. I knew they loved the song and believed the words.

As I recalled the lyrics now, I realized that my Heavenly Father was reminding me that I needed to take everything to Him—including my worries. He will carry our burdens and concerns—if we let Him—we are His children.

As you read each line of Joseph Scriven's song claim the verses for yourself by inserting a personal pronoun such as I whenever you read the word we. Allow God's promises to give you peace and comfort. Cast all of your cares upon Him.

What a Friend we (I) have in Jesus
All our sins and griefs to bear!
What a privilege to carry
Everything to God in prayer.
O what peace we often forfeit,
O what needless pain we bear,
**All because we do not carry
Everything to God in prayer.**
Have we trials and temptations?
Is there trouble anywhere?
We should never be discouraged —
Take it to the Lord in prayer.

Can we find a friend so faithful
Who will all our sorrows share?
Jesus knows our every weakness —
Take it to the Lord in prayer.
Are we weak and heavy-laden
Cumbered with a load of care?
Precious Savior, still our refuge —
Take it to the Lord in prayer.
Do thy friends despise, forsake thee?
Take it to the Lord in prayer;
In His arms He'll take and shield thee —
Thou wilt find a solace there

The Recess Bell Always Rang Too Soon

Kathrine Palmer Peterson

Sometimes as adults we are hesitant to enter a new phase of life. Like the changing seasons we must learn to enjoy each one for its value and beauty. We must enjoy each season of life to the fullest, not just exist through them.

I remember my youth and it's many pleasures. Those carefree days of health and vitality, sweet memories of birthday parties, sleepovers, Christmases, the first kiss, family vacations and Sunday school. We all have similar memories of our childhood. Yet, if we stayed in that mode and never took on challenges we would never achieve higher goals. Whether you choose college, marriage, family, career or all these choices, you first must initiate the move that will start you toward your goal and future.

After a loss it is even more important to have hopes, dreams and goals. This is a new season of your life.

When I need a little inspiration, I recall a valuable lesson I learned from a simple childhood game called three-man skip rope. One child held each end of the rope and swung it at a steady pace, while a third person attempted to jump in. The objective was to complete a jumping sequence without tangling or stopping the rope. I had taken my turn as one of the rope twirlers and recall the feeling of anticipation when my moment of opportunity to skip arrived. I recall the rope twirling, fast and high, as I readied myself to jump in. I swayed back and forth with the rhythm of the rope mentally preparing myself to jump when the rope reached the bottom of its rotation. As it started on the upward course I determinedly had taken action and had successfully jumped in. Of course, it seems easy now, but there was a time that the game held a certain level of difficulty. The older children I played with hopped in with such expertise that my own attempts appeared almost comical in comparison. How glorious it was when I, too, learned to jump with wild abandon as they did.

It was a thrill each time I successfully jumped in, exactly matching the cadence of the jump rope cycle. Once in, I was able to sing one of the many rhymes I had learned from my mother, sister, and friends.

I remember singing softly and then a bit more boldly as my confidence grew:

> I'm a pretty little schoolgirl,
> As happy as can be.
> I have a dark-haired boyfriend,
> Who is in love with me.

> I L-O-V-E, love him,
> And miss him all the time,
> I K-I-S-S, kiss him,
> And hope he will be mine.

Upon finishing the round I exited with the same exuberance as I had entered. This childhood game taught me that it was more fun to play than to watch, even if I was a twirler. And, if I took a chance to jump in, even if I failed once in a while,
> I could begin again.

As is true in life, regardless of whether I jumped or not, the recess bell always rang too soon. So learn to jump in. You may make a few mistakes along the way but you will, once in awhile, sing the song of celebration.

Persevere

Don't jump out of line in the parade because others have finished before you. Continue marching with zest to the beat of the drums, with honor, waving your flag — persevere until you know that you have completed your objective and can say to yourself, "Well done."

Fannie Roach Palmer

Chapter Three

Loneliness

Losing a loved one who was an important part of your life and who is no longer with you in this physical life can create an incredible imbalance to your life. The scales are fully weighted with grief and you struggle to bring equilibrium back into your life. You may be surrounded by people but still feel lost.

It is similar to the feeling I had when I stayed in a Boston hospital a few nights. The city was beautiful and packed with people on the streets hurrying to some destination unknown to me. I gazed out the window of the solarium and beheld the magnificent view of the skyscrapers against the skyline and the beautiful twinkling lights. I observed one tall building had a decorated Christmas tree on its rooftop. Oddly, something that should have cheered me made me lonely for my loved ones. Here I was in a city with over a half a million people and I had never felt so alone in my life.

Loneliness, we all know the feeling. How do we deal with it?

Donna Bradley, a young widow, describes loss and loneliness this way.

"You're never quite over it, just, unfortunately, used to it."

"I, too, can relate to the feeling of emptiness. It has been five years since my husband died in a horrific accident and I feel that my emotions occasionally play games with me. (I guess something like that proverbial emotional roller coaster we all speak about.) I feel most vulnerable and lonely on the occasions that I see many couples together, whether it is a couple celebrating their 50th wedding anniversary, or couples holding hands as they walk through the mall. I still have a feeling of anger and of being deprived of a contented life with a spouse. Even though I have reason to have those feelings, I can't help but feel sad and lonely for the other half of my life that is missing. All any of us can do is trust God for He has a better plan ahead for us."

In the following segments you will learn about Linda, a teacher who lives in Brooklyn. She candidly shares some of the most private thoughts and emotions that she experienced during the first three years of grief.

"How do you rejoin the world of the living?"

"Sometimes I think the only thing that keeps me sane is going to work everyday. I teach, and the term will be ending on June 28. The thought of spending eight weeks home alone talking to myself was so frightening that I agreed to teach summer school. If I know that I have a place to go to everyday, I can get myself up, dressed and out the door. I look forward to being with my class and my colleagues at school. But, as soon as I put one foot outside the school door, I start to cry. I cry all the way home and continue on and off through the evening until I take my medication (antidepressants) and fall asleep. It is not a restful sleep, nor a restorative sleep. And then, when I wake up the next morning, it all begins again.

I feel as though I am rapidly starting to become the proverbial anchor around my grown son's neck; it seems as though he can't have a life without me glued to him a lot of the time. I really don't want to hang on to my son so much, but I am afraid of being alone. I can be alone for short periods but then I start feeling sorry for myself and get frightened of the future and what will become of me. Everything is done in solitude—I eat alone, shop alone, walk alone, etc. I see a grief therapist once a week and that at least gives me another adult to talk to and gets me out of the house for a short time. When I am alone, the walls close in on me and I don't know how I will manage without Joel for whatever time is left for me. I don't really want to die anymore, although I wanted that in the beginning, but I honestly do not have the slightest idea how to rebuild my life. I'm not interested in meeting anyone and I already have three college degrees, so I don't want to go back to school. How do I rejoin the world of the living?"

"I haven't been hugged for real since Joel died."

"Donovan, my grandson, will turn three months old on Sunday. This little guy is the light of my life and I can't imagine my life now without him.

Every morning he greets me with a big smile and gurgles. I love his little head snuggled in my neck. In fact, since Joel died, that little baby is the only "touch" contact I have. He is the only place I get hugs and kisses.

Soon, I will forget what it is like to be hugged or kissed by anyone other than this infant. I used to go to a therapist who absolutely insisted on hugging and kissing each client when they left after their session. She said that a human being needs ten hugs a day to grow emotionally. She was so phony with her hugging and kissing routine, refusing to let me pass by her without subjecting me to her mandatory affection. I asked her to stop because I just couldn't bear it any longer.

People who actually care about each other enjoy the emotional acts of hugging and kissing. Being forced to hug and kiss as part of a therapy ritual is unfulfilling. I am currently two years plus ten hugs a day behind in emotional growth according to her. The kids in school sometimes run up and hug me, but other than the baby and the school kids, I haven't been hugged for real since Joel died.

We continue to follow Linda, and are now a little over two years into her grief journey.

"I think that now, at 25 months, I have only finally accepted that Joel is truly gone. I have always known he was gone, but the heart's acceptance is far slower than the head's. Over the last 25 months I have tried desperately to regain my former life, my former friends, the former "me." And, only now have I discovered and accepted that my old life is just not there anymore. I just wanted to retrieve everything that was so dear to me and so comfortable and so Joel.

Now, I've accepted that I'm going to be here without him for whatever time I am allotted and that I'd better do something with that time."

Linda now has reached her third year of grief and shares her insights.

"I just don't know how to begin this life, or where to find it."

"It has taken two years for me to actually want to control some of the aspects of my life.

The first year Joel was gone was a blur, with the exception of a few horrible events. I know I lived through it because I'm still here, but the days all slid into one another. All I did was work, work some more, come home, cry, sleep and wake up again to go to work. On the weekends I hibernated in the house and cried, or went to my friend's house and cried there. She divorced Joel's best friend about the same time Joel died, so we made the new "odd couple."

To give you an idea of the fog I was in, here is a typical story. Joel died in August about three weeks before the school term started. When the first year anniversary came around I had the same three weeks to pull myself together to get ready for the new school year. Some time around Labor Day, I went to my closet to check over the "school clothes" and move out the "summer hang-around clothes." When I started going through my closet, I discovered lots of new clothes with the tags and labels still attached. Obviously, I had purchased them during that first year, but I had no clear memory of having bought those clothes.

Now that the second year has come and gone and I begin my third year without Joel, I am trying to do more with myself than just work and cry. I have investigated widow support groups for younger widows and discovered that there are very few of these groups. I guess it is just assumed that widows and widowers will be senior citizens. This is a big misconception. I am mindful that I have to have a life that consists of more than Brian, Vikki and little Donovan and working two or three jobs. I just don't know how to begin this life, or where to find it.

After almost thirty years together, I've forgotten how to be a person without Joel. I know it sounds silly, but somewhere, they should offer classes to "suddenly single" people on how to make or find a life after having been married for so long.

When a person gets divorced, they are either angry or delighted depending upon the circumstances of the marriage and the divorce. But, in a divorce, the people have a choice in becoming single. They have the option of divorcing, staying married and being unhappy, staying married and seeing a marriage counselor, etc.

And, if you're divorcing because your spouse has left you for someone else, you tend to want to get out in the social scene to "prove" to yourself and your former spouse that "you've still got it." But, when you become a widow or a widower, you don't get a choice.

The hole in my heart feels so big I feel as though I am going to fall into it. Most widows or widowers don't want to jump into the social scene as fast as their divorced friends. First, we don't have to prove anything to an ex-spouse, and second, the emotional devastation is so great that socializing under those conditions isn't appealing.

I know now that I don't want to spend the rest of my time here all alone with just my son and his family. I am open to the possibility that I might, someday, have another relationship. But someday, not now. It just doesn't feel comfortable yet. I still feel married. Each of us wants to be in control of his or her own life and I used to think I had some degree of control. But, when you're faced with a sudden death, or even a death you've expected, you suddenly realize that the control you thought you had is all a farce and you have control over nothing.

This journey through widowhood is filled with peaks and valleys, as is the journey through any kind of grief. But, to borrow a saying from the 12 Step Program; "I'm not where I want to be, I'm not where I'm going to be, but thank God I'm not where I used to be."

Linda reached 3 years and 4 months of grief with a renewed spirit.

"The holidays around here took on a much happier tone this year as it was my grandson's first Chanukah and first Christmas. My son and I are Jewish and the baby's mother is Catholic, so little Donovan gets to celebrate both holidays. He just turned seven months old, cut his first tooth and is now walking holding on to the furniture. What a pleasure to see the joy of the holiday season through the eyes of a little one. With all the presents he received, he still wanted to play with the bows, wrapping paper, and empty boxes.

For myself, I miss Joel terribly and the celebration of Chanukah has not been the same since he is gone. I lit the candles only one night so far. When Joel was here, we lit them every night. But, back then, we were a complete family.

Now, the third Chanukah without him, the family still has that terrible sense of being incomplete. I know in my head that the family we are today is complete the way it is. It is just a different complete than it was when Joel was here, but it is still my family.

It is hard to fathom that three Chanukahs have passed without him. How he would have enjoyed seeing his grandson open all his presents. He would have absolutely enjoyed getting presents for him. I did that part for the two of us.

I do have some happy and exciting news—I have met someone really wonderful and special and he has become a part of my life.

Right out of the blue, I met Rob, a widower. I was undergoing some tests for a medical problem when I met him right here in Brooklyn. As soon as I started talking with him, I immediately felt as if we had known each other for years. There was such a sense of belonging and comfort. This man was there for me as I underwent all those tests and procedures, he treated me as if I was made of delicate porcelain and he couldn't do enough for me. We got engaged on February 14—he has four kids (yes, four kids!)—and we'll be married on November 17th.

He is a great big teddy bear of a man, 6 feet, 8 inches tall, about 290 pounds, but a real pussycat at heart. My first impression of him was that he was very intimidating and fearsome, so I hesitated to get to know him. I can only tell you all that I am glad I didn't stop at first impressions.

He is a wonderful, sweet, gentle, loving, and compassionate man. He is always there for me when I need a shoulder to lean on. He thinks I am the sun, the moon, the earth, and the stars and a girl can't get much better than that. I've met his kids, all the kids and grandkids have met each other and the families have hit it off well.

Even my sister and her husband met him. They found it a little hard to have dinner with us because they are so used to having Joel with me, but they made it through the evening. Rob is a wonderful man who makes me laugh, makes me sing, makes me smile that big, dumb smile we get on our faces when we are falling in love.

Here's another funny fact, his first wife's name was also Linda and she and I have the exact same birth date. Tell me that someone up there didn't arrange this. No, he isn't Joel and our relationship isn't like the one I had with Joel. But, I'm not his first Linda either, and our relationship isn't like the one he had with her. A second marriage is a lot harder than a first marriage and sometimes I find myself thinking that there aren't just two people in this relationship, but four. Our deceased spouses are with us all the time.

Everything I am today is due to the life I lived with Joel—everything good about me, as well as, everything not so good about me.

We both understand that whatever we do, wherever we go, Joel and Linda, our first mates, will always come along with us. We are both comfortable with that. So, a new adventure is starting for me and perhaps a new life with a new love.

This is a major step for me, even though I knew many months ago that I wanted to be part of a permanent, committed couple again. Now that it is here, I'm actually scared to death. But, for the first time in a long time, I'm happy again. I feel as if all the empty spaces have been filled up and I know that if I am happy, Joel is happy, too.

Joel and I were "beshert" which is a Yiddish word that roughly translates as "meant to be." Joel and I were "meant to be." One's "beshert" is that one person in all the world that is meant to be your soul mate, your partner in this life and all other's, the person God wanted you to be with. That is a "once in each lifetime" thing. But, maybe, just maybe, God pulled a few strings when He had Robert and me meet. To have been blessed enough to find a strong and deep love once in a lifetime is a gift from God. To be fortunate enough to find it a second time is a miracle."

Linda comments on her grief experience as she looks at it in retrospect.

"When I looked back on the words that I had written in the early stages of grief I was amazed. As I read it, I remembered "who" and "what" I was at the time it was written; how broken and sad I was. I had been fighting so hard to build a life, an identity that was my own. The turning point for me came when I stopped enumerating all the terrible things that had happened to me in my life and started to count the blessings God left me even though He took Joel Home.

I realized that I still had my son, daughter in law, and my precious little grandson. I also had a job I love and reasonable health. I knew that Joel would fully expect me to be strong enough to make it without him. In the early days of widowhood, someone (I don't remember who) told me, "The measure of your courage is not in the number of times you fall down, but in the number of times you get up again!" All of us who have "lost" and continue to get up again are truly courageous!"

Joyce is next to express her story, she is a fifty-eight year old mother and grandmother.

"I would like to have a life that is not so lonely"

"My husband has been gone for three years. I don't know how to become involved again or how to find a way out of my solitude. How do I make new friends? How do I build a life again? I do not want to meet "someone", I would just like to have a life that is not so lonely. I feel as though I am part of the living dead. I am just going through the motions of living.

The most purposeful thing I do all day is clean the house and take care of my dog. I need more in my life. Please help me."

(Joyce and the others in this chapter will find answers to their questions as they read this book, lean on their faith in God and learn from the wisdom of others.)

Maybe you feel like Anne, a young woman from Washington. Anne also speaks of her feeling of loneliness and searches for answers.

"I have lost part of my identity, who am I now?"

"How do I learn to rejoin the world? I've lost a big part of my heart and life.

My identity that used to be so entwined with my husband now has crumbled to dust. We were always together, now I am alone. How do I reach out for help? No one seems to notice that I am alone. How do I fill some of the emptiness that I feel? I have survived my husband's death, but I feel so lost and don't know which direction to go on my own.

Finding my way out of this abyss is a mystery. I hope and pray that someday I will find my way back to the living."

Louise is a woman who has a yearning to be needed and loved. She also proclaims that she has a lot to offer and, for her, marriage is a major desire for her future.

"I still have a need for companionship"

"My husband died at fifty-four, at a time when we were finally getting a chance to do all of the things we had planned to do: travel, fix up the house, and spend time on our boat.

Our children had all grown and moved out so they didn't need us as they once did. We were going to be a carefree couple again; or so we thought.

Now I am thrown into this unknown world of despair. I imagine my days now with no one to share my life. I, hopefully, have many years left and don't want to live those years all alone. I still have a need for companionship, someone I can love and who will love me. I need someone to make life fun again. I want to live life not just exist in it. This desire is strong and I trust the Lord that he has someone for me in the future. I need to know that it is acceptable to want to marry again.

My husband and I loved each other very much and were true to each other through all of our years of marriage. After twenty-six years of marriage he was still the love of my life and my best friend.

Because I have a desire to move forward, I want to make a new life for myself that doesn't include a life of being alone. I am concerned that people will think that I didn't love my husband.

I just want to have a life that is more desirable than the one I am living now. I want to love someone and have someone love me.

My loss is intense, as is my loneliness. My husband is gone and will never come back. I am here alone and know that I have to try to live what I have left of my life to the fullest; I can't live in the past any longer. I must make a plan for my future for whatever God has planned for my life—I will embrace it and work to make the best of whatever comes my way. I don't feel guilty for how I feel, but I do find it awkward to share with others what is truly in my heart, and to tell them of my dreams and hopes for the future."

Suzanne shares her story with us next, she is a loving mother of two daughters and she is unsure of her future.

"My heart's cry is, "I don't want to be alone!"

"My children's loss of their father is so different than the loss I feel for him as my husband. I feel their pain and am sorry for their loss, but I am affected by my loss in such a different way. One daughter is in college, and the other is in her last year of high school. They have their whole lives ahead: they have college, love, marriage, children, and wonderful futures to plan.

I know it sounds selfish, but I can't help think what is going to happen in my life. What do I have to look forward to now that Ron is gone? There are so many things we had planned to do with our lives.

I still want to do the things we had planned. He was both my present and my future. Now, I do realize that God is bigger than my sense of loss, but I have to be realistic. I have to decide what I want to get out of my life.

I know I need to pray for God's wisdom and His will. I can't accept that my life is over because Ron died. Next year when I am alone in this house it will be even worse.

What do I do with my life now? My heart's cry is, "I don't want to be alone!" I fear being alone. I try to continue my friendships with the couples we used to enjoy socializing with. But those friends seem to be distancing themselves from me. I've discovered that they fear having a single in their couples group. I now feel like an outsider in a group that was once extremely close.

They leave me out of the regular group plans and then make up silly excuses as to why I wasn't invited. They were supposed to be my friends. At least they were when Ron was alive.

I am not sure why such a change has taken place. It upset me enough to finally say to them, "Hey! Ron died, I didn't. I'm still here. I still need you people to be my friends, where have you gone?" Of course, this only made me more of an outcast. They didn't know how to cope with me any better than they did with Ron's death. I am bewildered and hurt. Maybe I remind them of their own mortality and how it could happen to them.

I pray that God will give me peace and help me to forgive those who have not acted as a true friend. I also pray that I will have the courage to make new friends, as I know I must."

Barbara, a formerly sociable person, now feels abandoned by her friends and shares her feelings of confusion and loss.

"I still need you to be my friend"

"My friends are deserting me, it really hurts to see all that we once had changing so fast. I'm trying to live with it but it is hard to accept. How can they just set me aside so quickly? I'm finding it hard to cope with this.

I'm feeling left out and really at the point of reverting back to the anger stage which I thought I had dealt with. I think this is a new and different anger. This anger is for the unexplainable loss of friends. I haven't done anything wrong so why am I being punished? How do I tell people that I still need them to be my friend?"

Jason is a handsome young widower with dark eyes that reveal a deep sadness. He explains his loneliness.

"Time only lessens the intensity of the pain, it doesn't heal it."

"My wife died almost two years ago. The loss I feel is incredibly fresh and intense. My friends try to convince me that time will heal everything. I can tell you that time will not heal anything. Yes, the intensity of the pain will subside, there are moments when I can think about other things, every moment isn't consumed thinking about her, missing her; but she is always there in the back of my mind. I pretend that I am doing well when I am with others—they expect it.

When I am home alone I can let my guard down and let my true feelings surface. The truth is that I miss her more today than I ever have. The loneliness is the same day after day, at times it is overwhelming: I eat alone, I watch TV alone, then I go to bed alone. I no longer have someone to laugh with me, to encourage me, to love me, to just be with me. There is no one for me to please.

She used to laugh so easily at my jokes. Those simple everyday precious moments are what make me ache for her. My wife used to say that if she died she would want me to get remarried.

What we had can never be replaced, but I do hope that there is someone out there for me, and that one day I can find happiness again."

Dana, once again, reveals some of her wisdom.

"The pain can't be over until the grief work is done."

"Just to get through one day, is about all I could manage to think about. I hoped to see the light at the end of the tunnel, because I just wanted the pain to be over. I realized that the pain couldn't be over until the grief work is done.

Grieving is a long, arduous process that involves a great deal of pain, soul searching, and faith. Grief counselor, Bill Webster, said something at my first meeting that really made an impression— he said, "The longest distance in the universe is the distance between our heads and our hearts. Grief is the process that helps us get to the point that our heart will come to know what our head already has knowledge of."

I, too, had isolated myself from the world. I sensed that my friends were uncomfortable whenever I spoke about my loss. I lost my feeling of dignity when I couldn't get out of bed and take care of ordinary things such as personal hygiene. Certainly in this condition I was unable to care for my daughter properly. Sometimes I had to actually hire outside help to come and entertain her because in that emotional state, I just couldn't handle the responsibility. My daughter was only three at the time her brother was taken from us."

Jane Burfield shares successful strategies that helped her survive a difficult day.

"Life should be lived, and should not be filtered for the rest of our lives through a dark, dark screen of regret and loss."

"Today is the first month anniversary of Mark's fatal car crash, and it is also our 26th wedding anniversary. I expected it to be an extremely difficult and emotional day.

I have survived this far by having several strategies that I thought I would share with others to help them face difficult days. I still have 6 hours and 20 minutes or so to go until I can put the day behind me, but I am hoping to get through it with as little grinding pain, and as many happy memories as I can.

I have begun going to a wonderful grief counselor. We had our second session on Tuesday, and I talked about some of the issues that might arise today—what I would be thinking about, and what I would be remembering. By talking about it then, it made today a little easier. I know I will have to face certain days that will be trigger points for grief.

The grief journey is a long and extremely painful one. Unless I think it can have a resolution, a moving on in spite of the pain of the loss, I doubt that I could remain as positive as I am. I was so fortunate to have a warm, loving, and caring relationship, one filled with joy, and silliness, and a sense of being cherished and of cherishing. I had that for 30 years with Mark.

I am so terribly saddened to think he won't be part of my active life for the rest of my life's journey, but he would not have wanted me to be consumed by my grief permanently.

I know I will miss his company, his laugh, his wisdom, and simply holding his hand on an evening walk. I know that I have to rely on my own judgment now, and I have to learn to be independent.

When you have the difficult days, the trigger days, the ones filled with dark thoughts and longed for memories, think of brighter days ahead. There will be a time when you will feel gladdened by seeing a tree return to life in the spring, or joy when you hear the laughter of a child. There will be memories to make as you share giggles with friends at a silly movie, or experience emotional parts of life that make you feel alive such as when your child is married, or is happy.

Life should be lived, and should not be filtered for the rest of our lives through a dark, dark screen of regret and loss. I need to teach my children how to grieve, while I learn myself. I need to show them that life can and does go on, and that joy can still be found in our lives. May all of you find peace, and acceptance."

Chapter Four

Healing Activities

How I Survived Grief
Fannie Roach Palmer

"My mother passed away when I was fourteen, and it was decided that life would be better for me in America with my sister, Susie. So I left my beautiful home in Nova Scotia, that sat nestled on top of a mountain and had spectacular views of the great Bay of Fundy. I left behind all that I truly loved: my father, brothers, caring neighbors, and teachers that had meant so much to me. Little did I know that my dear father would have only two more years on this earth.

Moving to a new country wasn't an easy transition for me, but I was grateful that I had been given the chance to come to such a great country of opportunity. I was determined to excel in school.

When I was old enough, I followed in my sister's footsteps and went through nurse's training at the New Hampshire State Hospital School of Nursing and affiliated at Mass General in Boston.

I met Edward Palmer Jr. here in New England and my life was never the same. I had found the most loving man and we married. My in-laws were wonderful Christian people. My mother-in-law took me under her wing and we shared a close mother and daughter relationship. She had six sons so she relished the thought of a daughter—I had lost my mother many years before, and considered my mother-in-law a special gift. God blessed me in so many ways by giving me an extended family.

Ed and I had a beautiful daughter, Elaine, then we suffered a miscarriage—we depended on our faith to see us through. We were blessed with three more children; Stevan, Kathrine and Bradley. Our family was complete and we had a wonderful life together.

As time progressed I lost more family members through a variety of circumstances including cancer, drowning, and heart attacks. I lost my father and all of my siblings, three brothers and my only sister.

My mother and father-in-law also went to be with the Lord along with two dear nephews and many loving friends. My life is richer for loving and from being loved by all of these gentle souls.

The most difficult day of my life was the day I lost, Ed, my beloved husband of 49 years, when he suffered a fatal heart attack. I, like countless others before me, found myself in an unexpected situation. The plans and dreams that Ed and I shared were painfully cut short—he was my life. He had worked his whole life to make our family happy, and I knew that I owed it to him not to waste what is left of my time on earth. And, although my life will be far different than my original expectations, I still have work to do, and I have purpose—and so do you. I give you this analogy as I relate it to my own life. Don't jump out of line in the parade because others have finished before you. Continue marching with zest to the beat of the drums, with honor, waving your flag—persevere until you know that you have completed your objective and can say to yourself, "Well done."

God has been my constant guide in times of sadness. Looking back on my life I can clearly see the footprints in the sand of God working in my life, and I am grateful.

His grace has seen me through the valley of tears and grief, and because of these trials I have emerged a stronger person—in character and faith.

The 23rd Psalm paints a glorious picture of God's protection as our Shepherd. My prayer for you is that God will lead you beside the quiet waters, and as a contented lamb in a green pasture, may you find rest. May God revive your wounded spirit, guide you in your path and refresh your faith. And even though you walk through the valley of the shadow of death, He will be your comforter—you should not fear evil, for he is with you always.

18 Key Points to Grief Survival

Fannie Roach Palmer

1. First, and foremost, lean on God for strength.

Praise God, know that He cares. Quiet your heart and mind, open yourself to Him, and draw your strength from His word. I derive enormous comfort from meditating on these verses in Ephesians that tell of God's magnificent love. Read this passage and reread it until it sinks into your being as a sponge would soak up the rain, let it fill your mind and heart until it is full—may the message revive you and give you hope. Ephesians chapter 3 verses 16-19 I pray that out of his glorious riches he may strengthen you with power through his Spirit in your inner being, so that Christ may dwell in your hearts through faith.

I pray that you, being rooted and established in love, may have power, together with all the saints, to grasp how wide and long and high and deep is the love of Christ, and to know this love that surpasses knowledge—that you may be filled to the measure of all the fullness of God.

2. **No matter what anyone tells you, realize that there is no correct way to grieve.**

There are no set rules that fit everyone, or every situation. There are general grief guidelines and suggestions, but ultimately, you decide what decisions to make and when to make them. Allow yourself time and space to sort out your emotions—use your own time frame—give yourself permission to grieve when you need to.

3. **Find support**

Become involved with a grief class or group where you will receive support. Many of my neighbors and community members also lost their husbands. We bake for each other, call, visit and uplift one another. Although our friendships have spanned many years, the bond we now share is solidified by our mutual losses. It is encouraging to see anyone in the group take a step out of grief. Each milestone that is overcome by an individual gives us all motivation to continue to find comfort, peace, and purpose.

If there isn't a grief group in your area, start one. You only need to start with one other person. You probably won't have to look far to find an individual or two who would like to go out to eat once a week or once a month or whatever schedule is acceptable.

Plan a gathering, it can be an activity as simple as going to the mall or having coffee and cookies or a prayer time at your own home. Some of my friends started a game time where they get together and play board games for a few hours. These gatherings serve a purpose. Of course, the main benefit of getting together with others that are experiencing grief is to form new friendships and nurture the old ones while offering an opportunity to fellowship. It also presents the opening to extend comfort to those who are newly bereaved, a prime opportunity to offer guidance and encouragement along with friendship.

You will find, at some point in your grief there will come a time when you will laugh again—it will not be because you have forgotten the pain of your loss, but in spite of it. Dr. Annette Goodheart made a perceptive observation when she noted, "In order to laugh, you must be able to play with your pain."

4. Learn to live without guilt, self pity or anger.

If you don't, you will never find contentment. Look for peace and comfort in God through the Holy Spirit. Read the Bible and look for verses of consolation and encouragement. Attitude is everything. Monitor your words and thoughts— are they mostly negative or positive?

5. Dare to dream

There will come a time in your life when you are again able to think and function rationally. Take time to consider what you want to do with your life—you hold the reins to your future. Continue to do something useful and don't waste a precious moment.

There once was a teacher who gave his students an assignment to write their own obituary, as they would want it to read someday. This lesson gave the pupils the opportunity to think about what they hoped the future held for them and what contributions they wanted to make during their own lifetimes. What this teacher was trying to instill in these young minds was that they could direct their future to a certain degree, but first they had to have dreams, goals, and plans. They had to know what general direction they wished their lives to take. Each student was required to decide how they wanted to spend their time and their future. Would they waste it or use it wisely? What choices will you make now?

Opportunity does knock, but you have to get up to answer the door.

Are you too old to learn from this lesson? The answer is up to you. How are you spending your time? Life is too precious to waste; turn that TV off and go do something useful. At the end of the day you need to know that you have done something during the day that has given you a sense of satisfaction and accomplishment.

There is nothing better to take your mind off yourself than to do something for someone else. There is a whole wide world out there full of people to love and to love you and your opportunities are endless. Don't waste even a moment.

I've known Louine Olson, a pastor's widow, for decades. She has been debilitated by rheumatoid arthritis and from countless operations so much so that she needs to be cared for. Through her pain this woman has remained cheerful and continues to inspire and encourage others through letters and phone calls; she is a prayer warrior.

When I realize how difficult and painful it is for her to write I am amazed at her spirit. She has had a ministry without even leaving her home. God has used her and she has been a living testimony to all who know her.

If you are fortunate enough to have your health, by all means take advantage of it. Help people who need to be encouraged: share your faith, be active, and challenge yourself to grow mentally, physically, and spiritually, daily.

Never stop learning. Explore places you have never seen, even if it is only the next town over. Make people an integral part of your day.

How do you know if your mission on earth is finished? Richard Bach wrote: "If you're alive, it isn't."

6. Discover your gifts.

In the New Testament we are taught that the Holy Spirit gives special gifts or abilities to all Christians. Develop your gifts for a deeper service. The fruit of the Spirit in Galations 5:22 are listed as love, joy, peace, patience, kindness, goodness, faithfulness, gentleness and self-control.

7. Don't make decisions you may regret.
Take time to assimilate all that has happened before you make decisions concerning matters that don't need to be attended to immediately. Take your time to figure out what is right for you.

8. Be open to new experiences and relationships.
There is a new tomorrow, work toward the brighter day.

9. Do your grief work.
Allow yourself the time you need to work through your emotions and your loss. Take whatever time you need to grieve. Don't let anyone berate you for grieving over the loss of a loved one. Grieving is a normal process, healing takes time.

10. Be a friend.
A true friend is a great blessing, especially one you can cry in front of and still be loved. Reach out to someone else, be a friend.

11. Be busy every day.

Keep your mind occupied with positive activities.

12. Serve God

Help people when you can, if you can't help the multitude then help one person. Mother Teresa said, "If you can't feed a hundred people, then feed just one."

Reach out to someone today. Call, visit, or write to encourage someone who needs it.

Some individuals become incapacitated by grief so much so that they can't even get their own meals or clean their home. Look around you when you visit a grieving friend to see what you can do. Be a doer of the word, be a friend who quietly gets tasks done in a discreet manner. Discern what it is that you can do that will be comforting and practical. Invite the person to your home or stay with them during the initial shock.

13. Remember this, you don't get over grief, you learn to live with it.

Create a memory table where you can display pictures that are full of wonderful memories. I created such a display and included every family member. The whole family finds comfort in those happy memories. Let those memories warm your heart. We don't have to forget the past to move into the future.

14. Keep your mind positive

A verse that sums up how we should focus our mind is Phil. 4:7 Finally, brothers, whatever is true, whatever is noble, whatever is right, whatever is pure, whatever is admirable—if anything is excellent or praiseworthy—think about such things.

Remain positive; resist becoming negative or bitter. Guard yourself against thoughts or actions that are joy stealers.

15. Talk about the deceased—it is healing.

Memories are a special gift from God. These mental pictures offer a way to carry our loved ones with us at all times. When we need to, we can take out these memories as if we were leafing through a treasured photo album. They are forever in our minds and hearts. Talking about a loved one and reminiscing are healing activities.

16. Set goals, make a plan. Your life is not over, don't use the death of someone else as an excuse to waste your life.

Helen Keller, a woman of great courage and wisdom, overcame what would have been insurmountable obstacles for most individuals.

She said, "Self pity is our worst enemy and if we yield to it we can never do anything wise in this world."

A sure way to help yourself emotionally is to help someone else.

There will be times when you need to rest and sit quietly to think and to let your mind catch up with reality. (I know because there were many nights I just sat in the dark) and there will be times when action is required. An Indian proverb tells us to "Call on God, but row away from the rocks." Use the knowledge, strength, and gifts that you possess to steer your life in a positive direction. Don't allow yourself to drift into the rocks of despair and hopelessness. You can sit around waiting for the phone to ring—you can mourn hopelessly for the life you used to have—or you can decide to take action in your life and give your life purpose.

My daughter, Elaine, used to plan her own parties. It was always difficult to plan a birthday party for her because she wanted to have control of her own event. She knew exactly what decorations she wanted, what music would be the best, and planned all of the activities. She invited her friends weeks ahead of time and took great joy in the planning and anticipation of the coming party.

Of course, each party was a great success because of her enthusiasm and the care she took to make sure that everyone had a good time. Elaine is still that energetic, fun-loving person today. She has always celebrated life, moment by moment. So take Elaine's example—life is too precious to waste.

When you are able, plan activities of your own that will keep you involved and busy.

17. It is important to do something nice for yourself.

Set aside time daily, to do something that will give you comfort, or bring you happiness. Find an activity that gives you joy and then do it— whether it is gardening, reading, walking in a park or visiting with friends—add a little pleasure to your life each day.

18. Celebrate life.

I realized that my husband had worked his whole life to make others happy. I could not undo his life's work and his wishes by not making my own life useful and fulfilling.

It was with a great sense of fulfillment that I watched my grandson, Jeremy, graduate from the University of New England, with his Master's degree as a Physician Assistant. It was with joy that I watched another grandson, Justin, receive his high school diploma. I've enjoyed hockey games and concerts that my grandchildren, Justin, Brandon and Tyler have participated in. I am also thankful for being a part of the birthday parties and events of Tammy, Jakob, Billie, Emily, Kayla and all the family members. With great love and delight I relish every precious moment with each of my children and their mates and families.

I am grateful for my children because they are loving people, and for my son, Steve, whom I depend on the most. Family, faith and happiness is what my husband and I worked for, and for my husband I observe and celebrate each moment and wish that he could also experience these events. Celebrate life, it is too precious to waste. I give praise to our Maker for all things. I thank you, Lord, for your great love. Praise His Holy name."

Diane Crandall has been a teacher for more than 30 years. She developed her own grief guidelines that she shares in her classes with students of all ages. As a former student in Diane's program, I can assure you that these guidelines along with Fannie Palmer's 18 Key Points to Grief Survival, made a significant difference in my life.

There is grief work to be done.

Guidelines from Diane Crandall 's
Dealing with Grief Class

1. Study God's word, seek wisdom and guidance.

2. Even in times of duress, learn to be grateful. Each day write down at least one thing that you are grateful for. Keep these lists to look back on when you are feeling low.

3. Don't make major life changing decisions right away. Some individuals change locations immediately only to discover that the decision was a huge mistake.
Give yourself every opportunity to think through major decisions. Don't rush into something you may regret in the future.

4. Make a list of family and friends who are important to you and who you are important to. Stretch out your service to people you don't know. Volunteer where there is a need such as a hospital, school, soup kitchen, local church or community outreach. Don't waste life, make a difference, you still can. If you are homebound, become a prayer warrior, call to encourage others, write letters, knit, or bake.
Everyone has a talent to use.

5. Learn to say no. There will be many demands on you and you will need to know when you are about to reach your limit. Draw the line to conserve your strength.

6. Make a wish list of things you would like to do and then begin to make those wishes come true. Make a list of 50 things you want to do and then start checking them off as you complete each one. And, as you check items off your list, add new ones.

7. Begin a new venture, travel, take a course, learn a new hobby, or start a project. This may be one of the hardest steps, especially if for the first time, you do it alone. Try to get a supportive friend to join you.

8. Don't think that you have to please everyone; you will be setting yourself up for disappointment. There will always be individuals who will be critical of how you are grieving; either it is too fast for them or too slow.

   No one knows how you feel or what time frame is best for you to grieve. Be strong on your own path to grief recovery. No one can dictate how you should feel. This is a personal journey.

9. Exercise

10. Don't let yourself become housebound. Live life to the fullest for yourself and for the memory of your loved one. If there is life in you, use it and make it count.

11. Surround yourself with people who really care about you.

12. Volunteer, be involved in life and show concern for those around you. The more you help others the better you will feel.

13. Channel your energies where it will make a difference in the lives of others.
   I taught the *Dealing with Grief* class in order to share what I had learned. In the giving I received new insights, new strength, and new friends. Also, I created a lesson for a grief video, *After the Tears, A Gentle Guide to Help Children Understand Death*, in memory of our loved ones.

Each person needs to choose a project that is meaningful to him or her. Some people have founded new charities or begun their own organizations.

Make something positive come out of the sadness that you feel.

14. Change your routine. We all get set in our ways with our own personal rituals. Now may be a good time to change your regular routine, especially around the holidays.

15. Make a place of comfort in your home where you can go to relax and have peace and quiet. This can be your healing environment. Use this place of tranquility to pray, meditate, read, or listen to soothing music.

16. Make a change in your home to give you a lift. Paint or wallpaper a room, put out flowers and plants, change the pictures or move the furniture.

17. Hang onto the memories and items that you need to and let go of ones you don't.

18. A big morale booster is laughter. Remember to laugh. Remember to smile.

My Adaptation of the Original 7-Ups of Life
Kathrine. Palmer Peterson

1. **Get Up** – Make the decision to have a good day. "Today is the day the Lord hath made; let us rejoice and be glad in it." Psalms 118:24

2. **Dress Up** –A cheerful look brings joy to the heart, and good news gives health to the bones. Proverbs 15:30

3. **Speak Up** – My mouth will speak in praise of the Lord. Let every creature praise his holy name forever and ever. Psalm 145:21

4. **Stand Up** – For Jesus and your convictions.

5. **Look Up** - To the Lord. My son, give me your heart and let your eyes keep to my ways.
Proverbs 23:26
 Keep your eyes riveted on Him. Let Him guide and protect you.

6. **Reach Up** –Remember when Peter tried to walk on water in Matthew 14 and he saw the wind and was afraid. He began to sink and he cried out, "Lord save me!" Matthew 14:31 tells us that immediately Jesus reached out his hand and caught him. He is always there for us—we only have to reach up.

7. **Lift Up** - Your Prayers. "Do not worry about anything; instead pray about everything."
Philippians 4:6

  Some of the journal keepers asked to have their discoveries added to this section. They wanted to share their own personal survival tips. Here are their mini-lessons on dealing with grief and life.

Kimberly, in her early 20's is a young single woman who lost both parents. Her advice is this.

"Never give up on your dreams. I had to give up on mine while I cared for my father. He encouraged me to go back to school and now I am working toward my degree. I then plan on travelling to other countries. I am forcing myself to work hard to achieve these goals. I know I can make it."

Jill lost her husband.

"My advice is learn to adapt to your new life. You can't move on until you accept the reality. Life still feels like it is spinning exceedingly fast, and I am moving in slow motion. I have come to accept my situation—it's my first major step to healing."

Linda lost her husband.

"One of my survival rules is to make each day count by completing something that I couldn't do before. I applaud myself for new accomplishments no matter how small they may be. I need to know at the end of the day that I have done something that has made a difference.

To me, healing has been in very small increments. I couldn't stay in the depressed state that I was in, so I have taken a little bit of control of my life. I am beginning to move forward. The grief work for me is difficult, but I am finding it beneficial and truly healing."

Gina lost her son.
"Ask yourself this one question, 'Are you doing the best possible things in life that would make the person you lost proud of you'?

I know my son was proud of the way we were involved in his school and outside activities. My husband was a scout leader and baseball coach; they enjoyed these activities together. My husband and I continue to volunteer at school functions because we know he would want us to continue to contribute time to his school and classmates. It is difficult to face the other parents, teachers, and coaches, but we are doing it for him."

God Blessed the Creatures

God made the animals
that move along the ground.
It's the story of creation
in Genesis it's found.
He said, "Let the water
teem with living creatures,
and let birds fly above the earth."*
God formed all living things,
each has importance and great worth.
He knows every bird in the mountain,
and every creature of the field.**
He watches over His precious flock
He is our Shepherd, Rock and Shield.

Kathrine Palmer Peterson

Gen: 1:20a
**Psalm 50:11 paraphrased

Chapter Five

Pet Tales of Love

The Journal of American Geriatrics Society stated that pet ownership in the golden years of life has a positive effect on seniors' physical health and mental well being. They went on to say that caring for a dog or cat can ease the loneliness of the elderly, as well as provide ample opportunities for physical activity that bolsters overall health. And they contend that petting the pooch does more than just keep you fit. The researchers of this study concluded that the nurturing aspects of pet care gave older people a sense of purpose. The added responsibility in their lives encourages them to be less apathetic and more involved in daily activities.

Also, a major benefit of owning a pet is that they provide companionship to those owners without family and support systems, which helps them remain emotionally healthy during times of crisis, as compared to their non-pet owning counterparts, the study said.

If you have ever owned a pet you will understand and identify with the special love and bond that humans and pets share. These connections can be especially helpful for children and adults who are grieving. Some studies indicate that owning a pet can help lower blood pressure, heart rate, and anxiety levels for their owners.

Pet Tales of Love is a special chapter that I felt needed to be a part of this book. It doesn't matter if a pet has fur, feathers or fins, two legs or four, they all add joy to our lives.

Many individuals expressed their love for their pets and told me that their animals had a significant role in their grief recovery. Perhaps you will identify with some of these stories as you remember a few of your favorite pets. May you think back on those faithful animals of the past and smile as you reminisce.

The Other Side

Vernon C. Grounds,
Our Daily Bread

Many years ago a doctor made a house call on a dying patient, who asked, "Doctor, what will heaven be like?" The physician paused, trying to think of a helpful reply. Just then they heard the sound of scratching on the closed door of the patient's bedroom.

"Do you hear that?" the doctor asked. "It's my dog. I left him downstairs, but he got impatient and came up here looking for me. He doesn't know what's in this room, but he knows his master is here. I believe that's how it is with heaven. We don't know what it's like, but we know that Jesus will be there. And really, nothing else matters."

The Bible gives us a few faith-strengthening glimpses of what life will be like beyond the closed door of death. We know that heaven will be a place of radiant splendor (Rev. 21:23). We know that it will be a place of reunion as we meet again those whom we have loved and from whom we have been parted for a little while (1 Th. 4:17).

We know that there will be "no more death, nor sorrow, nor crying." (Rev. 21:4).

But above all, when we get to the other side, we will rejoice because Jesus is there, and we will be with Him forever.

Dove Lewis Pet-Assisted Therapy Program

The Dove Lewis Pet Assisted Therapy Program in Oregon, works to alleviate the stress and pain individuals are experiencing by using animals as a healing part of therapy.

Pet assisted therapy is a successful program because of the dedicated individuals who have the heart and compassion to help people and animals. Maybe you are an individual who can make a difference in a similar manner as the people in the Dove Lewis program. The trained personnel in the program define pet assisted therapy as "animals helping people to help people."

The animal handlers are a group of caring individuals who share the love of their own companion animals with others in a facility setting. This takes place in many different environments with people of all ages. They work in nursing homes, children's hospitals, hospice situations, schools, and adult day care. Some animals take walks and play with adolescents struggling with difficult issues while in treatment. Others provide stroke patients with something worthwhile to reach for over and over again, helping them to re-establish a range of motion as a part of physical therapy.

By offering warm and furry friendship, some facilitate people in severe depression to reach out beyond themselves. Each animal offers acceptance, unconditional love and elicits smiles and joy. The program has proudly used a large range of animals from dogs, cats, birds, bunnies, llamas, miniature horses and even a few chickens and ducks—but they are rare since farm animals usually do best in an outdoor setting. Dogs and cats are usually the first choices of the Pet Assisted Therapy partners.

The handlers attend classes to learn how to interact and respond to the various situations that might be encountered in nursing homes, hospitals and possible health hazards associated with these visits. They also learn the proper procedures of protocol when visiting.

When the classes have been completed, the handlers meet with the Program Director. They, along with their animals are evaluated for suitability in the program.

The new handlers are then assigned to a facility and generally make a couple of visits with a mentor who is experienced in Animal Assisted Therapy. Handlers find it rewarding when they connect with the facility residents and staff and often become a part of the family as they go about their work.

The Bond

Geraldine and Curt Von Ahn
Dove Lewis Pet Assisted Therapy Program,
Oregon

"I had the most amazing experience one night with my Therapy Dogs, Kyle and Scott, both Golden Retrievers. We had gone to a local hospital on what started out as a personal mission to visit with our one-week-old nephew. He was recovering from surgery in the pediatric wing. Our visit ended in a soaring confirmation of the benefits and truths of the human/animal bond.

A two minute walk from the car to the hospital room rapidly turned into a half hour meander as we were continuously stopped by hospital visitors, staff and patients who needed to pet the two Golden Retrievers or simply speak to them and make some kind of contact.

Upon arriving at our destination and beginning our visit with our nephew and his family, we were soon distracted by a six year old boy (we'll call him Tommy), clutching his mother's hand, IV tubes dangling from one arm and swathed in a too-large hospital gown.

The child had stopped by our open door and was gazing at the dogs so we walked into the hall for a visit. After some chatting and lots of dog petting, the mother asked her child if he wished to continue their therapeutic walk around the hospital hallway. Tommy hesitated and then gently shook his little head and pointed to Kyle. I quickly changed gears and asked them if they would like for Kyle to walk the halls with them and got a quick "Yes!"

Off we went, down the hall, Tommy lightly resting his hand on Kyle's back. Soon we met a noisy knot of child patients, most with tubes, IV stands and other hospital paraphernalia attached to them. I realized that the child with us was slowly growing taller as he swelled with pride in his canine companion. As we approached the other children, to their "oohs" and "ahhs", I decided to keep this as Tommy's special moment and told the children that there was a second dog on the floor and, if they waited patiently, he would be along soon to visit with them.

Upon returning to our nephew's room Tommy gave the dog a gentle hug and then he hugged me. His mother smiled and thanked us. I then dispatched my husband with Scott, our second Therapy Dog, to visit the eager children that were waiting down the hall.

While visiting with the children, a nurse approached my husband and asked if he could make a special visit to a particular little boy. This little guy was only three years old and had been in a serious accident suffering extensive injuries.

As my husband and therapy dog, Scott, walked through the doorway to the toddler's room, a cloud of despair lifted and smiles broke out on everyone's faces. Carefully, Curt and Scott approached the bed and Scott gently reached his massive head up and rested it on the blankets of the child's crib. It was a frozen moment in time for that family who had suffered so much. They were able to express joy as they petted the Therapy Dogs. We contemplated later that the child would probably talk as much and possibly more about the "doggie who came to visit me in the hospital" as he would about his more painful experiences there.

This started as a story of the human/animal bond. What I learned is that, in order for me to truly experience and live the truth of that wonderful relationship, I had to let go of a lot of control over my animals and learn to work more fully with them rather then try and control them.

You must understand that when we are out with the dogs, whether shopping or sight-seeing, Kyle is a dedicated "sled dog", who normally pulls at his leash and complains loudly that we just aren't walking fast enough or far enough for his tastes. Scott is an expert in leaping to his feet unexpectedly and sticking his huge paws out, pestering for people to shake his paw and pressing his head into them for petting. Such an embarrassment!

Such naughty behavior! This has been my "I need to be in control of this situation" type of thinking. As a puppy raiser for Assistance Dogs destined to work with people with various disabilities, I have always felt that my task is to teach the dog to stay totally and completely under my control as we go about our training and daily work.

I wanted them to look to me for guidance on commands and behaviors and that remains to be true for that aspect of my work with canines. An Assistance Dog needs to focus totally on their human team mate and ignore all distractions while performing its' duties.

However, I have had to spend some time retraining Kyle and Scott to have a more relaxed attitude in their dealings with people and to make some of their own decisions about who to visit, who to trust and what actions should be taken during the visit. It makes a huge difference during a therapy visit if the animal willingly, and with some enthusiasm, makes the decision to initiate interaction with any one patient or schoolchild. It makes the person feel wanted, liked and appreciated. It's part of what we are trying to accomplish.

Last night, I finally realized that although I had carefully trained the dogs, I had not spent enough time retraining myself.

I was so used to being the one in total control and so proud of the fact that I had carefully maintained Kyle and Scott's Assistance Dog program commands, that I forgot to retrain myself to the different needs and techniques of working with a Therapy Animal. I forgot that the world did not end if they were allowed to make their own choices about which direction to walk down a hall, which room to ask to enter, which person to visit and which to pass by. I forgot that they might have a very good reason for breaking a stay command or sticking a paw out to a particular person. They have a lot of love to share."

"We needed something to fill the empty hours at home."

Mark B.

"Shortly after my wife's death, I decided to purchase a puppy for my three children. Mike, my youngest, is only seven and the oldest is fourteen. It was Mike that took his mother's death the hardest. He appeared to be the most bewildered with the whole new life without his mother. He and his mother were close since she did not have an outside job and was able to spend plenty of time with him. We live close to a park and they enjoyed visiting it every day that it didn't rain. Things changed after her death, the house was too quiet, and the hours ticked by minute by minute. I took the batteries out of our clocks because I found that noise deafening. I couldn't stand the tick, tick, tick. I never remembered our house being so quiet. It was then that I decided we needed something to fill the empty hours at home, so we picked out a beautiful, white, miniature poodle, that we affectionately named Snowy.

The children have enjoyed laughter again by watching and caring for Snowy. The puppy loves to sleep in the children's rooms, and this has brought comfort to them during the quiet and dark time of the evening after they have settled down.

Of course, Snowy can't take the place of their mother, and that wasn't the intention, but he does help ease their pain and gives them something to care for, hug, pet, and love. This is healing and calming for them as well as for myself. Snowy has been a great addition to our family."

"Goliath Brings Laughter to my Life"

Ginger S.

"I need Goliath, my German Shepherd, so I don't have to be alone. He is great company and gives me a sense that he is guarding the house. He brings joy to my life; we enjoy hiking, camping and just hanging around. Recently, we went camping for a weekend in the White Mountains of New Hampshire. I found a beautiful campsite and we settled in.

Goliath has always had a strange habit of stealing pieces of my clothing and carrying them around in his mouth; this particular camping trip was no different. Unbeknownst to me, just before our walk he had grabbed a pair of my underwear. There we were parading down the road, me happy to be on vacation and proud to be walking my beautiful dog. Goliath was behaving like his usual playful self.

Little did I know that he was showing off my underwear to the whole camping community. I had noticed a few people chuckle as we walked by, but it wasn't until a nice looking gentleman stopped me to comment on Goliath's size that I was made aware of his choice of toys. Needless to say, I quickly grabbed the underwear and my face matched their color—bright pink!"

Now, I'm always sure to check his mouth before we take any more walks.

"The Day of the Dog Show Brownie Disappeared."

Elaine Palmer Frissell
Animal Hospital Manager, Massachusetts

"As far back as I can remember I have loved animals. As a youngster I was known for my strange menagerie of pets, and would regularly rescue any wild or tame creature that had been injured or needed assistance. To this day animals are an important part of my life. Because of my job as an animal hospital manager and through my own experience, I know that pets can be an integral part of a human's life. The animals that I see are considered as loving companions to their owners as well as playmates and protectors.

Since childhood I have owned an assortment of animals that included: horses, ponies, cats, dogs, and birds. I always found a sense of satisfaction in caring for each one. Animals can offer comfort and joy to anyone blessed to own them.

I share this next story with you so that you will understand the importance an animal can have in a child's life; and the devotion this special dog had for an old farmer.

When I was growing up, I owned a brown dog, named Brownie. He was an average dog of uncertain breed, but to me Brownie was the best dog ever. One day it was announced that our neighborhood would be having a dog show within a month and all the pets would have to obey certain commands to compete. I knew right away that I would enter Brownie.

Every day after school I worked with Brownie teaching him hand commands. We practiced for hours, over and over—sit, stay, and come. He was an intelligent dog and picked up the commands quickly. My young heart was delighted at the progress he had made and I was sure we would win a ribbon.

Brownie used to slip away to go to the neighbor's cow barn at milking time. He savored the activity and clearly made an excellent farm dog.

A distant neighbor, farmer Blake was elderly and suffered from a bad back that made it a chore for him to get around, let alone round up his cows.

Brownie actually was a tremendous help to the old man, because he would run to round up the farmer's cows with ease, knowingly guiding them toward the barn to be milked. This job he did with pleasure, and farmer Blake always rewarded him with a bowl of fresh warm milk. It was clear that Mr. Blake also loved my little dog.

On the day of the show I had groomed Brownie until his coat was shiny and free of tangles—this ordinary housedog looked like a potential winner with his head held high and his beautiful tail in a flume of browns and reds. I hurried to ready myself for the show—a crisp shirt and slacks would look just right, I imagined.

When I returned to the steps to get Brownie I couldn't believe my eyes—he was gone! I was devastated, all that work and no dog to show. All those hours of obedience lessons wasted. I searched everywhere for him as time was quickly running out. A friend of mine stopped by on the way to the show. I had helped train her beagles—she saw how sad I was and offered me one of her dogs.

When we arrived at the show I recognized all of the animals from the neighborhood and a few new ones. I scanned the grounds, Brownie was nowhere in sight.

The event proceeded quickly class after class. Some dogs ran off chasing other pets, others were curious and so involved in looking around that they just sat or stood without obeying any commands. None of the dogs measured up to my Brownie.

Most of the classes had already been shown when I looked up to see Brownie happily trotting down the road. Only he no longer was spiffy — I tried to brush the muck, mire, and twigs out of his coat using my fingers as a comb. To me he still was the best animal there, regardless of how dirty he appeared; he had plenty of heart.

I know Brownie knew farmer Blake needed him first, and he decided he had to be faithful to the old farmer. He had been "working" the cows at the farm and he smelled like one.

Thankfully, the judges allowed me the opportunity to put him through some of his paces—sit, stay, come. He obeyed each command instantly. To my delight he placed that day—maybe they gave me a "gift" of a ribbon but, at the time, I thought he deserved every inch of that prize."

Trasher's Lucky Day

Elaine Frissell

During the fifteen years I've managed the animal hospital, I've seen quite a few amazing stories—one of my favorites is the story of Trasher. The circumstances in this tale touched my heart as I realized how God could change the direction of a life in one instant. In this particular story, two burly men with tender hearts and a truckload of compassion saved a helpless little kitten.

While we were busy one day at the animal hospital, the Sanitation workers across town were on their usual round picking up the bags of trash and throwing them into the back of their truck where a powerful crusher pulverized the waste.

This day appeared to be like any other as they moved from one house to the next. They threw the bags in the hopper and watched them as they were quickly pulverized. The two men on this particular crew worked as a well-oiled team and didn't waste time lingering at any one stop. Their job consisted of one man jumping from the truck, picking up the bags and tossing them into the back of the mammoth dump truck while the other man drove.

Incredibly, just as the crusher was about to be activated, the fellow at the back heard a small "meow." "Stop" he instructed the driver. Then he yelled, "I think I heard something in the trash." Quickly he searched through the smelly trash—through old banana peels, coffee grounds and soiled paper plates—and there in the middle of it all was a tiny little creature. "I don't believe this, I found a kitten! " he shouted.

The thoughtful Samaritans brought the kitten to the animal hospital and told their incredible tale of rescue. After hearing the harrowing account of the kitten's narrow escape, I nicknamed the tiny survivor Trasher. He quickly became a celebrity when word of his rescue was circulated.

That day, little Trasher was headed for certain death. Yet, instead he was saved by caring individuals who took the time to intervene when they heard the little cry for help. Trasher was such an adorable little kitten that one of the technicians at our hospital adopted him. Today he is living a full life, happy, well fed, cared for, and best of all, loved.

When considering adding a new pet to your family, please go to your local animal shelter first. You can make a difference in the life of a pet and in the process you will discover that they will enrich your life."

"It was as if God sent me this puppy to help me through this heart-breaking loss."

Joy

"Shortly before my mother died, I got a Golden Retriever puppy. I had a strong urge to get a pet during my mother's final days. The puppy was three months old at the time and so very cute. I would bring Goldie with me to visit my mother at home. She would pat Goldie, and I know she found comfort having her by her side. We had many pets as I grew up over the years—mainly because my mother enjoyed them so much.

During my mother's last days, the puppy brought so much comfort and happiness to us both. I am a person of strong faith and believe that Goldie was a special gift to us during a time when we needed love, and a happy diversion from our situation. Goldie helped me get through the most difficult time of grieving. "

"Faith knew just when to give me that extra special attention."
Ricki

"After my father passed away I was feeling lost and alone. While out riding one day I came upon a hand written sign at a run down home that said "puppies for sale." I knocked on the door and was led into the kitchen where there was a cage with one tiny puppy sitting in the back. It was the cutest little thing and didn't make a move or a sound—it just looked as if it hadn't been loved or held—it was in sorry shape and appeared mal-nourished. I discovered it was a female Yorkie and knew then that she would be coming home with me. I decided to call her Faith because it would take a lot of faith to see us through our struggles.

She weighed only a pound and felt like a feather when I held her. I could feel every rib as she lay on my lap. It was a struggle to keep her alive, but through diligent feeding and care she pulled through.

I had such a hurting heart over the loss of my Dad, being able to love Faith and care for her gave me comfort. I know God led me to her, for her sake and my own. Faith, the pup, has brought so much love to our household.

She has given me barrel loads of love from the first moment I picked her up. When I've cried, and had down days, she has been there, looking at me with those big, loving eyes and stayed close to me. She knows just when to give me that extra special attention.

I would recommend that if you love pets and have the time to give them love and a good home, that you consider a pet of your own. They will enrich your life and bring you many years of joy, especially during times of bereavement. If I had not had Faith, I'm not sure what I would have done. She has provided comfort, love and certainly hours of entertainment when I otherwise would have been alone. Faith has given me reason to laugh and smile even through the tears."

"I feel less alone and vulnerable at night."

Joni

"I have found great comfort in my pets. I'm a bit like a frightened child at night—I hate being alone. I am comforted in the fact that one cat sleeps on the bed with me each night and guards me.

The other cat and the dog find it more appealing to sleep in the living room and wander in occasionally. I feel less vulnerable when they are in the house."

"Alexis, my dog, is a joy and a true gift from God."

Karen Alexander

"My dog's name is Alexis but we called her Alex. Actually, she was Terry's dog. We got her at a flea market. I used to tell Terry that Alex took after us. Stubborn like him and sweet like me. He would answer, "I think that it is the other way around."

Alex is a very quiet dog. She only barks when absolutely necessary, only howls when the fire alarms go off. When Terry was on life support in another city Alex howled every day. How did she know? Alex was crazy about Terry and she liked me, but she really belonged to him. When Terry died it was hard to look her in the eyes. She looked so sad. But since then she has been my solace, especially since my mother died. She makes me laugh.

When I wanted to just crawl in a hole or stay in bed, I knew I had to take care of her. She is comforting at times, when I cry she tries to jump into my lap—this makes me laugh.

When we go for a walk, I take her and sometimes she takes me.

I have a picture of Alex on my desk at work. I am located at an appointment desk in a medical office. I use a picture of my dog, Alex, because it makes me happy, and it also is there to cheer up the little children who are in the waiting room.

One particular day while Terry was sick, I was terribly down. Just to make conversation I showed the picture to a patient (an adult). He looked at the picture and said, "She's a Christian dog."

I said, "What do you mean?" He replied, "See, she has a cross on her chest." I looked at the picture and the symbol of the cross jumped out at me. Never before, until that moment, had I noticed the cross. I took it as a sign that God was with me just as He had been the day we picked her out. Rather, He picked her out for us. So you see, she really is a joy, a true gift from God."

"My face ached from laughing, and I experienced a feeling of release and relief."

Joslyn

"A long time had passed before I realized that I had not even smiled, let alone laughed, because of my grief. Then one day my sister's family was visiting. I had put some extra cake and sandwiches on the table to pack for them to take home. We had stepped outside for a moment and when we walked back into the kitchen we caught our dog, Barkley, licking the sandwich plate clean.

He looked at us with his big eyes as if to say, " What? Those sandwiches weren't for me?"

We laughed so hard that we bent over clutching our sides. That was when I realized that this was the first time I had really laughed in a very long time. It felt good. Now, when I look back I realize that in the beginning I felt guilty for having happy moments—so I suppressed them— but I have learned that laughter is good for the soul and a healthy part of healing.

I no longer feel guilty when I laugh, though sometimes I feel sad that I can't share the laugher as I used to. After I've laughed I usually have a bittersweet moment or two of sadness as I remember my love and my loss, and then the missing sets in again.

It has been a year and a half now and I cherish the fact that I can reminisce and laugh over the happy times we shared together. James is my favorite book in the Bible. I am comforted when I read James 1:12 Happy is the person who remains faithful under trials.

"Chopin-the-Bird sings cheerful songs all day."

Donna Bradley

"My friend, Christina, nearly went to pieces when she had to put down her dog, Lucy. I couldn't figure out why she was so upset, she acted as if it was a close family member or friend. (Don't get me wrong, I have pets too.)

About a year later, I found out that the dog was originally her mother's dog and she had taken ownership of the dog when her mother passed away. She told me at that time that it was the last piece of her mother's life, and she felt like she was grieving for her mother all over again.

At the time of Bruce's death I had, and still have, my two cats—George and Molly. George was Bruce's favorite cat, and he is mine too. He has quite the special little personality.

Now, after experiencing my own loss, I see how difficult it will be to lose my pets. George and Molly were present with Bruce when he died. When I came home that morning, the place was too quiet. The bedroom door was closed, the cats were in the room with Bruce. Normally at the sound of the door unlocking, they would have been pawing at the door to get my attention to be let out for their breakfast. When I opened the door to the bedroom, it looked like Bruce was sleeping. The two cats were both sitting beside his body as if they were guarding him, but initially I didn't perceive it as odd.

They never made a move to run out of the room for their morning kibble. They just stayed with him. Now, since we're on the topic of pets, the story of these two intelligent cats gets rather interesting. For the first two weeks or so, I slept at my friend's house. As soon as the sun went down, I had to get out of my condo. I couldn't stand to keep that room in darkness, and it took me months—seven or so—before I could sleep with the lights off.

The first few times I actually slept back at my condo my two pussycats nearly drove me crazy. Talk about spooky. The two of them would sit beside me with their little cat faces hanging over mine, every time I opened my eyes they were looking at me. Then they would paw me, and swat me, and meow and carry on like they were afraid to let me fall asleep. George, still to this day, claws back the covers on Bruce's side of the bed, as if he is looking for him. It took about a week or two before they would settle down and let me go to sleep, the poor wee things.

George was obviously not himself, he would lay by the front door for months and months, and followed me everywhere. He is usually independent. Even Molly's company would not help. Five months after Bruce died, friends of ours gave me a lovely canary. That canary brought my George back to life. George lies beside his cage, and will fall asleep while the canary sings and sings. It is so sweet.

Now Molly is another story, and it gets very interesting here. She would retreat under the bed in the spare room. When she went into my room, the room Bruce died in, she would leave accidents in there, sometimes she would lie under that bed too—she wouldn't bother with any of us.

Sometimes I would find her under the bed covers. She would stay in the bedroom and not come out for anything besides food, or to use her cat box.

This went on for eleven months. I tried everything under the sun. I swatted her with a broom once, which I am not proud of, but I was losing my mind. I used a water spray bottle and I would yell, no, when she did it (though she was so sneaky, I could never catch her in the act) and I would reward her when she didn't do it. I tried everything to correct the problem.

Two months after Bruce died, I painted that room. One month after that I tore the bed down, but the pieces remained in the bedroom for eleven months. I steam cleaned the carpet after I painted the walls. I tried everything to get her to stop her bad behavior. I found the situation disheartening.

I knew the situation couldn't continue much longer. I was probably going to have to find her a good home, which really tore me up, because I had rescued her from the Humane Society. I was all for rescuing animals, not sending them away. Then when I least expected it, something changed.

Eleven months after Bruce died, I took the bed parts out of the bedroom, and got rid of them altogether. I was preparing the room for the arrival of my new bed—finally. You must realize this is nearly one year after his death. Then, just like that, Molly stopped the incessant behavior. Imagine a cat holding memories like that for nearly a year.

That is when she started to socialize with people again. She began to hang around me, play with George and she discovered we have a new Birdie. She stopped hiding out all day. I could not believe that such an innocuous decision to remove the bed from my condo completely was going to be her turning point.

Now the home is so wonderfully peaceful, my two cats are happy, especially Molly. The sweet bird sings cheerful songs all day long. That bird has been such a blessing around here. For newly grieving people I highly recommend getting a lovely bird, you can't ignore the pleasant feeling they invoke when they sing their melodies. I couldn't imagine a life without pets. George, Molly and Chopin-the-Bird have been great.

Incidentally, it is now nearly two years since Bruce died, and Molly is still behaving like a good sweet pussycat."

"My pets have been therapeutic."

Deonna L.

"In regards to the discussion about animals helping individuals through the grief process I have this to say. I had three cats at the time Albert passed away. My oldest cat, the one that Albert got me for my birthday fourteen years prior, was the one I felt mourned with me.

I remember coming home and all I had left were his tennis shoes, billfold, and watch. I sat on the couch and the cat rubbed all over the shoes. She jumped up next to me and I remember telling her he wasn't coming home. Somehow I knew she understood. She spent the next month sitting in his recliner and looking at the door and crying pitifully.

After the month she ventured back into the bedroom and sat facing the wall where the crucifix from the funeral was hanging. If she wasn't hissing at it, she was staring at it. That also lasted a good month. I know she mourned for him and as much as she was hurting, she would instantly run to me if she thought I was crying. All three cats did that. They would come up to me and get real close to my face and watch for the tears. I don't know how many countless hours I spent that way.

I know they certainly helped me on some difficult days. They comforted me when they came up to me and tried to touch my tears with their paws, and then they purred until I stopped crying. They were trying to help the best they could. I think any pet can grieve for the loss of their owner and companion."

"Little Girl would put her paw in my hand as if she were human."

Fannie Roach Palmer

"When my husband visited the animal shelter he was going to pick out one cat that was yellow and reminded us of our previous cat. He and my daughter saw the perfect kitten sitting in the back of the cage, and as far as kittens go, he was rather strange looking. He had a pointy face and an independent spirit. As a matter of fact, when the attendant opened his cage door he bolted for the door. While waiting for the helper to process the paperwork, my husband, Ed, noticed a kitten that was in trouble.

It was a tiny little calico kitten that had its front paw caught in between the cage door. The little kitten was shivering because of its size and a tiny blanket that had been placed in the cage for warmth had become entangled in one little claw. My husband inquired about this malnourished kitten and discovered that it had been the runt of a litter and had been taken away from its mother too soon—it needed special attention to survive.

Ed had a tender heart and couldn't resist the pitiful little meows as the kitten pleaded to be held. Consequently, they came home with two kittens, both a bit of a misfit. Both needed love and attention desperately.

My daughter took Sylvester, the yellow kitten, and we kept the smaller kitten and named her Little Girl. With tender loving care our Little Girl grew to be a loving cat. She received much affection from our family and she delighted in bringing home her mice and depositing them on the steps for all to see. Birds were a different story. I would run to rescue the hapless creatures and the speed of my action most often worked out in saving its life. To my joy she didn't pursue bird hunting to any great extent.

Little Girl's favorite spot was resting between my husband and the side of his chair. She would be content for as long as he sat there. She loved to play in a paper bag and would rest for long periods believing she was well hidden from the world. Even in old age she would jump in the air and play with several toys she had throughout the house. So much joy was derived from Little Girl and our lives were greatly enriched from having God's lovely creature.

After my husband's death I was alone in the house except for Little Girl. She felt the emptiness too, and would search the house for Ed. Her ears would perk up when she heard something—she chose to lay on one of his shirts when he no longer was there to sit in the chair with her.

Little Girl was a comfort to me as we sat together on the couch. She put her little paw in my hand as if she were human and knew she would be a comfort.

I thank God for all of His precious little creatures, and am grateful that we had the opportunity to have a cat, that was so full of personality, for eighteen years."

Lost in the Woods of Maine

Kathrine Peterson

"It has been my observation that owning and caring for a pet offers benefits to children and adults of all ages. I remember the fun and companionship my dog, King, provided. He was a dog that was loyal, protective, friendly, and intelligent. He used to enjoy the excursions with us as we explored bubbling streams, fallen stumps, the Maine woods, and the creatures that lived in them.

One day, on one of our great explorations, my younger brother, Brad, and I went too far and became lost. We could no longer hear the traffic or any sounds that were familiar to us. We only heard the quiet peacefulness of the woods and the birds and bugs that had made their home there.

I began to get slightly fearful. I prayed that God would guide us out of our situation. It was then that I noticed that King wanted us to go in a certain direction. Like a scene out of a Lassie episode we both said, "Let's go home, King, find home!"

King took off in a hurry and we gladly followed him to the path that led us home. We arrived at the open road at dusk—safely. He knew which direction home was, and we only had to follow him.

As with God, when we are lost, we only have to follow him to find the way to his son and heaven.

*F*ind solace in friends and family,
find peace in the word of God.

Elaine Frissell

Chapter Six

Rainbows and Butterlies

Because we all see life through our own set of values and circumstances it was hard to assign a particular definition to the extraordinary stories in this chapter. Some will call them a comforting happenstance, or coincidence, while others will assert that they are a special gift from God; a sign, a blessing, or even a miracle. Whatever you call them these extraordinary events brought solace to the individuals who experienced them.

It is clear in Deuteronomy 18:11 that we should not get involved with people who conjure spells, or mediums, or spiritists, or people who call up the dead.

I believe that God allows us to find comfort through His creations. He gives us relief through tears, grief, emotions, dreams, nature, friends, family and, of course, His word and the Holy Spirit.

We begin our unusual stories with *The Miracle of the Vigil,* by Dr. Jane Robertson Westerfield.

The Miracle of the Vigil

Dr. Jane Robertson Westerfield.

"On Friday morning, November 5, as the sun rose over the ocean at St. Simons Island, Georgia, my mother, LuReese Watson Robertson, quietly yielded her spirit to God's eternal care. The week before had been a time of prayers and tearful good byes for our family as we watched her slip away. In the hours I spent alone by her bedside, I talked to her even though she could not answer.

Somehow I believe that she heard me as I thanked her for being such a wonderful wife, mother and grandmother. Since there were some indications that she was aware of what I was saying, I made one last request of her. I said: "Mama, when you get to heaven and find Daddy (my father had died in 1992,) please find a way to let me know that you are together." She did not reply and I continued my vigil during her final hours on earth.

In the moments after Mother died, I gathered her belongings and prepared to return to her home to join the rest of our family. However, I decided to go down to the beach for awhile to be alone with my thoughts.

It was a cool, crisp day and the sun was beginning to warm the air as I walked on the beach alone. As I stood looking at the ocean waves caressing the sand, I noticed two butterflies off to my left. Never have I seen two butterflies just alike, but these appeared to be identical and even more unusual, they flew so close together that their wings seemed to be intertwined! I watched entranced as the butterflies flew very close to my face, hovered for a few seconds and then flew away together.

Since my parents' Christian faith was strong and real, I knew that this was God's way of letting me know that they were alive and together with their Heavenly Father.

What better way to grant my request than to allow me to see two butterflies, the symbol of eternal life, as I stood alone in my grief? May God grant to all who grieve the knowledge that "those we have loved and lost awhile" are safe, happy and well with God and His Angels."

Our Main Comfort is Derived from His Presence and His Word

Lee

"God does use all sorts of things—a card, a spoken word, a near-accident, a rain storm, a rainbow, a hug from a Christian brother or sister, a cloud formation, a dream, the sweet song of a bird and many natural things to comfort the oppressed. Our main comfort is derived from His presence and His Word. God offers us this assurance in 2 Corinthians 1:3 *Praise to the God and Father of our Lord Jesus Christ, the Father of compassion and the God of all comfort, who comforts us in all our troubles, so that we can comfort those in any trouble with the comfort we ourselves have received from God.*"

Message in the Clouds

Kathrine Peterson

"Shortly after my father's death, my mother and I were driving home from town. Since we live in Maine we travel various country roads. One particular area we pass through overlooks a beautiful hill with corn fields, a pond and a large forest—local children slide and toboggan down the hill in the winter, nature lovers enjoy the wild deer and turkeys that appear at dusk.

On this particular day my mother and I drove by this location and as always glanced at the view. To our utter amazement we noticed brighter than normal white clouds that perfectly formed a cross.

The clouds weren't in the shape of a T; they formed a perfect cross. We also noted that there wasn't a wind as we usually have since we live on the coast. As we stared in awe, the cross remained in perfect formation, with straight exact edges. There wasn't another cloud in the sky, and from this vantagepoint we could see for miles.

As Christians, the cross holds great significance to us. My mother and I discussed the unusual formation and what it meant to us. We believe that Jesus died for our sins and rose again. We have security and take comfort in the knowledge that some day we will see him and our loved ones in heaven. We were grateful that God let us see His beautiful clouds that happened to be in the form of a cross. We felt as we would if we were staring at some of God's other great creations such as Niagara Falls or the Grand Canyon. He is the master and creator of it all. We were reminded of His great love for us that day knowing that Dad was safe in the arms of Jesus; this experience was an unexpected comfort to us."

The Mourning Doves of Peace

Linda Alexander

"When Tom died I was devastated. I went home and before anyone got there I went into the solarium and I asked Tom to just please let me know he was all right. I felt his presence standing in the doorway.

There had been friends coming and cleaning for the past two weeks and the solarium floor had been cleaned twice in the last week. I looked on the floor where I sensed Tom was standing and there was a feather.

My two sisters-in-law arrived and I told them what I had found. Tom's sister said that the feather was that of a dove. We sat there talking and a few minutes later she looked out the window and there was a dove sitting on the log right outside the window by me. It sat on that log for a half an hour, just sitting and occasionally looking in the window at me. Whenever I feel as though I can't stand the situation any longer, I hear a dove cooing.

A week later when everyone had gone home, I was by myself for the first time. I was lying on the bed crying and I heard something on the gutter outside the window. Then I heard a dove cooing. Every time I go out on the deck I can hear a dove or see one in the yard. It has been a great comfort to me. I have found other feathers since that day and they always bring a bit of joy to my day. I still hear the doves cooing almost every day. As a matter of fact, they have taken up residence in my Blue Spruce tree right outside my solarium.

I discovered a curious fact about the doves from my pastor. I always thought they were called Morning Doves but their true name is Mourning Doves. It seems appropriate for them to be here since doves represent peace."

Pennies Appeared Everywhere

Lynnie

"This may seem crazy, but my late husband always had collected pennies in a jar (long ago cashed in.) After he died, it may have been my imagination, but for a long time, I would see pennies here and there in my house on the floor and then here and there wherever I went. It was a source of comfort for me. I believe that God gives us comfort through signs and wonders—why else would Jesus have healed so many and done so many miraculous things while here on earth? "

God sends us all kinds of signs of His mighty love

Doris Duplantis

"God sends us all kinds of signs of His mighty love.

First, He sent His only Son, Jesus Christ to save us while we were yet sinners and didn't deserve it. He sends warnings of bad weather like dark clouds, lightning, and thunder so we can come into safety.

He sends signs of new flowers to tell us spring is coming. Birds to sing beautiful melodies in the wee hours of the morning—grass, seeds, and plants to show how He cares for each of us.

Then in Fall He sends signs of the coming, shorter days, welcoming cooler weather from the summer heat.

He feeds the birds, would He not feed us also, this is a sign of His caring love. He allows us to become parents, to duplicate ourselves. He provided legs to walk, voices to praise Him as He so richly deserves, eyes to read His word, ears to hear these words spoken; noses to smell the sweetness around us. All these He has planned and made for His glory, so we can give Him the homage He deserves (our love and obedience.)

Sometimes He speaks to the deep recesses of our heart if we're in tune to His magnificent voice. He also allows us to have heaviness in our hearts, then reveals why. "

The Day the Clocked Stopped

Helen Peterson

"My husband and I happily celebrated our 30th anniversary with our children, family, and friends. As a special gift we received an anniversary clock that we kept in our kitchen so that every time we looked at it we would be reminded of our love and those we love.

The year my husband died the anniversary clock stopped. I changed the batteries and moved it to another location, I did everything I could to make it work, but to no avail.

I thought that there must be some meaning as to why our special clock stopped. Was it because we would never celebrate another wedding anniversary? I left the clock in the kitchen because of the sentiment associated with the piece.

I went through the first year in a blurry haze. My life, my love, my husband, my reason for getting up in the morning was taken from me. Time, our wonderful time together was gone forever: no more times of laughter, no more time of sharing our lives together, no time to plan our retirement years and no more anniversaries to celebrate.

Then, remarkably, one day as our anniversary date drew near I heard the familiar tick, tock, tick, tock of the anniversary clock.

For one whole year the clock had remained silent and now, as suddenly as it had stopped, it started to function again. Tick, tick, tick. Time moves forward, and love is timeless."

Grampa Read Me a Story

Bradley Palmer

"One day my wife, Mary, and I were in the van driving home with our daughters Emily and Kayla. Emily was happily sitting in her car seat and suddenly exclaimed, " Grampa read me a book last night!" In unison, my wife and I echoed, " Grampa?" Three-year-old Emily shook her head to affirm that we had heard her correctly. "Yes, Grampa," she replied. Mary and I exchanged puzzled looks and were a bit bewildered because my dad had died before Emily was born and the only living grandfather she knows she calls Papa.

My father loved his grandchildren and when a visit ended he would hug each one and say, "Remember, Grampa loves you." Emily had never heard these loving words.

What we would soon learn would astonish us more. When we arrived home we took out a group photograph that included my father. Emily had never seen this picture before. We held the picture in front of her and asked her, "Emily, who read you the story last night?"

Without hesitation she pointed to my father's image and said, "Grampa read the story." We were amazed how quickly she identified my dad and called him Grampa with such recognition.

There was one more odd incident that occurred that particular week. Emily had been having a difficult time going to sleep; she was restless and night after night we had tried to comfort her to no avail. The night she said Grampa had read to her had been the first night that she had quickly settled down. She started out a bit restless and then settled in and went into a sound sleep. We were a bit baffled until Emily elaborated on her story. She said, "Grampa read to me, then he said he was tired so we went to sleep." This seemed to explain why she had been comforted more than any other night.

Emily had described the event the best she could—and quite accurately described my Dad's personality. Dad used to pretend to be tired if it helped one of the little ones settle down to take a nap. We were pleased and felt blessed that Emily found great comfort and joy in remembering her story time with Grampa.

I relate this story to you as it happened. I can't explain how a child—not yet three—could identify a picture of a person she had never seen, and correctly name the person she saw by his correct and favorite nickname "Grampa." Whatever the reason, we are comforted that our little girl had a chance to have her Grampa read her a story."

The Assurance of Immortality

Dr. Jane Robertson Westerfield

"After my father, Bishop Frank L. Robertson, (Brother Frank) retired from the episcopacy of the United Methodist Church, he was asked to be the founding pastor of a new church on St. Simons Island, Georgia, Wesley United Methodist Church at Frederica.

He eagerly accepted the challenge, inviting many families to join the new congregation. As would be expected, these charter members of the new church worked very closely with my father and were devoted to the church and to him as their pastor.

One family, Karen, Tom and their children, were enthusiastic workers in the new church until Karen was diagnosed with cancer. She struggled valiantly against the disease and was often admitted to the hospital for treatment when she reached a crisis. On one occasion when Karen was particularly ill, she was admitted to the Intensive Care Unit. She remained unconscious for several days. One day she awoke smiling as she saw her husband, Tom, standing next to her hospital bed.

"Tom, I have something incredible to tell you!" Karen exclaimed.

"What is it, Honey?" he asked anxiously.

"I've been to Heaven!" Karen answered. "It's the most beautiful place you could imagine. I saw Jesus and some of my family members who have died. They wanted me to stay with them but I guess it's not time for me to go there yet."

Karen paused for a moment. "Is there something more you want to tell me about Heaven?" Tom inquired.

"Yes, there is something I don't understand. I saw someone else in Heaven."

"Who was it?" he questioned.

"I saw Brother Frank in Heaven with Jesus and he held out his arms to me. Why did I see Brother Frank in Heaven?" Karen asked.

Tom was stunned for a moment but he knew he had to tell Karen the truth.

"Honey," he said gently, "Brother Frank died two days ago while you were unconscious. That must be why you saw him in Heaven."

What an assurance of immortality this was to two families. To Karen and Tom as they faced her death a few months later and to our family when they shared this story with us. How grateful we are that God assures us that there is a place for us in the house not made with hands, eternal in the heavens."

He is Alive

Dr. Jane Robertson Westerfield

"Some friends gave my parents a beautiful plant that native Georgians call a "tea olive." It has lush green leaves and when it blooms, the tea olive is covered with tiny white flowers that have a sweet fragrance much like gardenias.

Mother was especially thrilled with her new plant and took care to see that it was watered and properly fertilized. She waited eagerly for the sweet, white flowers to bloom, but each year she was disappointed because it never bloomed. She kept the plant in the house for awhile, then moved it out to the patio hoping to encourage it to bloom. Still the plant remained green and lovely but had no flowers. Mother tried everything she could think of, but for five years, the tea olive did not bloom and she finally gave up, thinking it would never blossom.

One Sunday morning in December our family was experiencing deep sorrow. My father, Bishop Robertson, had gone home to his Heavenly Father. I awoke after very little sleep that morning, and walked into my parents' living room; then I opened the drapes covering the patio doors to let in the morning light. I could not believe what was before me. There, in the frosty December air out on the patio, stood the tea olive plant covered with beautiful tiny white flowers! I called my Mother in to see it for herself.

"I can't believe that tea olive is blooming! She exclaimed. It has not bloomed since we got it five years ago!" We looked at each other in amazement as we realized that it was a sign. God was letting us know that there is life after death and that my father was happy and well with the Lord whom he had loved and served throughout his earthly life.

The tea olive's fragrant blooms lasted only one day—after that it never bloomed again. But that one day, a grieving family received a message of comfort that our loved one was truly alive."

Changing of the Seasons

With God as your rock you will have the ability
not only to experience the changes of the
seasons of life, but to embrace them for the
gifts that they hold.

Kathrine Palmer Peterson

Chapter Seven

Comfort and Peace

The chapter on comfort and peace had to be one of purpose. Therefore, I consulted with Pastor Stan Rockafellow who is affectionately known by the congregation as Pastor Stan. He has been a minister for 34 years and began his first pastorate in Michigan where he served for three years. He then felt led to plant new churches and moved to New Hampshire with his family where he established four more churches. The last church he started is located in Maine where he and his wife, Donna, are actively serving God each day. Not only did they leave a trail of new churches, they established a history of saved souls and changed lives.

Because of his experience and wisdom, I asked Pastor Stan to write a piece that would be of comfort to the many individuals who would read this book. He graciously answered this request by writing *A Prayer to God* as a prayer for those who are grieving.

He then asked Don Staples an elderly man in his 90's who also has a heart for the Lord and a special gift with poetry to contribute a prayer.

After I read the prayers of Pastor Stan and Don I was moved as I felt a peace that only comes from God.

My prayer is that you, dear reader, will also experience the same sense of comfort, peace, and hope as you read the collection of inspirational prayers in this chapter.

You will also read heartfelt prayers from women of faith such as Fannie Roach Palmer, Donna Perkins, Diane Crandall, Gail Sicard, and Willie Pearl Scott who are special prayer warriors. Relax and settle your mind from worry as you read and meditate on the words and their meanings.

The highest purpose of prayer is to deepen your relationship with Him, and through Him in prayer you will truly find a greater peace and hope.

Remember that even a brief prayer can help you begin a new day, not alone and in your own strength, but with God.

Prayer lifts your wearied spirit and provides you with wisdom, strength, hope, and comfort through God's grace. What better way to begin your day than in the presence of the Lord?

Let Our Hands be an Extension of Your Love

Kathrine Palmer Peterson

Dear Heavenly Father,

We come to you praising your Holy name. We also come with heavy hearts of loss. Father, please minister to those who are grieving, show them your peace. Where there are burdens, uncertainty and emptiness we ask that you provide renewed strength, direction and wisdom. Fill us with knowledge of your love that will sustain us through our grief. Our hearts are aching and our bodies are weary from sorrow. Heal us dear Lord from the constant pain of loss. Lessen the sorrow and increase the blessings of memories of all those who grieve. Supply friends and family to physically comfort and encourage those in need. Let our hands be an extension of your love as we endeavor to comfort others. We know that you are the creator of the heavens and the earth and all that are in them. You designed the ocean's tides, the movement of the stars and every cell of all living creatures. We know you are with us through our pain and care for us.

We may not understand, Lord, why our loved ones were taken, but have faith knowing that they are safe in your arms. We take comfort in the verse of Ecclesiastes 4:2 when it says: And I declared that the dead, who had already died, are happier than the living, who are still alive.

I thank you, Lord, for each individual who shared their story or wisdom with us so that we may have a better understanding of grief, hope and peace. Bless each one who reads this and minister to their spirit, lift them to a new level of understanding and peace.

In Jesus name.

Amen

Prayer for Strength
Gail Sicard

Dear Father God

I ask you to strengthen my hands that are weak and my knees that are feeble. Fear has surrounded me at every turn. I come to you refusing to let it master me. You are my Master, my trusted Friend, my Confidante, the Lover of my soul. Father, you alone know the limits of my earthly frame, but I am reaching beyond into your heavenly realm.

In that place I ask you to soak me in Your love, peace, hope, joy, and encouragement until I have Your heart and the mind of Christ. I ask you to remove any root of bitterness, and any unforgiveness due to a lack of understanding on my part. I want to enjoy your sweet Holy Spirit and the taste of the heavenly things to come. I need you, Lord, to give me a fresh, new confidence in the plans and purpose You have for my life. I need to see your hand move in the land of the living.

I love you Jesus.

In Your precious name.

Amen

He Restoreth My Soul

Fannie Roach Palmer

Dear Lord,

We praise you and pray that those who read these prayers will find comfort in your mighty love. And through the 23rd Psalm may they find reassurance of your glorious presence. May they find peace in the knowledge that your love is true and everlasting and that you will meet their needs. Please, dear Lord, heal the sick and brokenhearted, help those who are experiencing financial difficulties, mend broken relationships, and bring families together and closer to you. May those who are grieving find comfort beside the quiet waters, and as contented lambs in a green pasture find rest. Revive their wounded spirit, Lord, and guide them in their path and refresh their faith. And even though they walk through the valley of the shadow of death, give them faith to ask that your will be done. We praise your holy name and thank you for your loving grace. We will not fear evil, for you are with us always.

In Jesus precious name,

Amen.

Prayers by Willie Pearl Scott

I lost my dear mother, Barbara Lee Scott Harris, on March 17, due to colon cancer. While I have an older brother and a younger sister, and nephews and nieces, I don't have children of my own. My mother, sister and I were a "threesome" and did so many things together. I was overwhelmed with grief after her loss. My mother was saved, so I know where her soul is, and she taught Christ to her family. My sister and I are saved. We accepted Christ 23 years ago.

Lord Heal My Heart

Dear Heavenly Father,
   Truly my heart is heavy today, and my eyes are full of tears. I cannot stop crying. I feel as though my most precious possession has been taken from me, and I will never find it again. I need you to come in and heal my heart, to restore my soul to peace.
Please refresh my spirit with your love, wash me anew in your joy, and surround me with hope everlasting. Let me see with a spiritual eye, those things that you have prepared for your children.

Soothe me now, oh Lord, and comfort me as only you can. Caress the hidden recesses of my soul. Help me to delight myself in thee, and in thy word. Restore my joy, Oh Lord! These blessings I ask in your name, and I will be careful to give you all the praise, the glory and the honor. Amen.

Lord, I Thank You for Fond Memories

Dear Heavenly Father:

Thank you for waking me up this morning, clothing me in my right mind, and giving me the activity of my limbs. Thank you for giving me a wonderful mother on this side of glory. Now that you have taken her home to be with you, I thank you for fond memories.

I thank you for the memory of her smile; it is the light for many a gloomy day. Thank you for the memory of her kisses and hugs, I feel them when I truly need strength.

Thank you for the memory of her words of guidance, they pointed me to you and continue to help me make right choices in life. Thank you for the memory of her love because it continues to warm my heart. Lord, I thank you for fond memories of my mother, because fond memories turn my tears to smiles, and make each day more worthwhile. Amen.

Comfort and Strengthen Us

Diane Crandall

Dear Lord,

We come to you with aching hearts and troubled minds. We praise you for being a sovereign God who knows our every thought and weakness and has the answer to our every problem.

You lived on earth as a man and experienced all the emotions we feel right now and you have promised to "never leave us nor forsake us". So we place ourselves in your loving care. You told us we could call you "Abba Father" (Daddy) and so we ask you to wrap your arms around us, to comfort and strengthen us, to still our troubled hearts and to surround us with your perfect love.

We thank you for all you will accomplish in our lives.

In Jesus name we pray. Amen. Heb. 13:5 Gal. 4:6

Healing Grace

Donna Perkins

Father,

For each one who may be reading this book; seeking answers for the pain of their own personal losses, whether it would be a loved one, a job, a physical inability, or whatever it might be, I ask your grace to be poured out upon them. Take the confusion, the questions, the fears and the hurt and use it all to draw them to yourself that each one might come to know your love for them. That they might experience the healing grace that only you can provide.

In the quietness of the night, when fears and uncertainty so often settle in, cause each one to be so aware of and to crave your presence. When so many places, scents and sounds bring overwhelming reminders, comfort them and bring to their mind moments of joy and laughter.

Above all, lead them to hope in Christ and the confidence that You have not left them or that You are a God that is unapproachable but rather that You are a Friend who sticks closer than a brother. I thank you Lord for all that you are doing and I lift each one, though yet unmet, to you for safekeeping.

In Christ's Name.

Prayer of Praise

Don Staples

We thank you, Our Father,
that there is no height or depth
or breadth or measure to your Grace,
and your mercy knows no bounds.
You set up Kingdoms and take them down again.
You heal all our diseases,
and heal the broken heart.
You forgive nations, who transgress your laws,
and bring revival to those
who repent and seek your face.
Please Lord, Heal our land today,
and comfort our people.

A Prayer to God

Pastor Stan Rockafellow

Dear God,

I turn to you in this my hour of grief, because you are creator of life and light. Your holy Bible tells me that at the sound, and command of your voice, you brought the world into existence. You said, "Let there be light," and all darkness fled its presence. You sent your holy son, Jesus Christ, into my dark, sinful world, and through His death and resurrection, life and light have come to all who believe.

O' God, you know my heart and the ocean of pain I am feeling. My soul is consumed, and overwhelmed with the darkness of grief, a grief that seems greater than I can bear.

I ask you now, as I pray, to please speak once again, this time to my heart and its darkness. Give me understanding so I can believe and receive your son; give me strength so I can go on with life. Let me see you so that I can see the path you have chosen for me.

In Jesus Name
Amen.

*Cherished memories
are like roses,
their fragrance lingers
and fills our senses with
sweet perfume.*

Fannie Palmer/Kathrine Peterson

Chapter Eight
Bonus Chapter
Excerpt from:
Write from Your Heart,
A Healing Grief Journal

Work Through Grief
the "Write" Way

In this book you will notice that instead of pushing you to "get over" the loss of a loved one, you will be encouraged to embrace and record the memories you hold of that special person.

Part of recovering from grief is remembering all that is close to your heart and learning to live in harmony with those memories. Writing in your grief journal will guide you toward this recovery.

Welcome to *Write from Your Heart.*

The following remarks were gathered from experienced journal keepers to illustrate the benefits they encountered through journaling.

- "When I looked back at the journals I had kept I was amazed at the progress I had made through my grief. I didn't realize how depressed I was at the time. Thank you for providing this opportunity through your guided journal."

- "I didn't know what to do with the sorrow, fear, and regret that had built up inside me. Writing about them helped me to release them."

- "Holidays are hard to face. A week before a particular holiday I would write the emptiness I knew I would feel during the upcoming celebrations. I also wrote down what I could do to alleviate some of the stress. This activity helped me defuse a portion of the heartache that I felt on the actual day."

- "I am finding peace through writing and prayer."

WRITE FROM YOUR HEART
A Healing Grief Journal
A 4 week journal
for personal or group use.

What is a Grief Journal?

Working through grief is a necessary part of the grieving process. Our mind realizes the circumstances around our grief but it takes longer for our heart to accept the loss. One method for helping the heart to mend is to use words that will connect our mind and our hearts, our thoughts and our emotions by allowing the experience to flow onto the pages of a journal. Once written down they can be read, acknowledged, prayed about and dealt with in a positive manner. It is through this journal that you can learn to let go and let God lift you to a level beyond your circumstances.

A grief journal is a work of love that you will create by writing your feelings, thoughts, and emotions as you have experienced them. It is an opportunity to write about your loved one. It is also a place to draw strength through prayer and to find victory over grief.

Writing serves many purposes—it can be creative and therapeutic. It can also provide valuable historic family information for future generations or it can be a personal diary that you compile just for yourself.

Many groups have found that keeping a journal can be a powerful tool when dealing with a particular challenge—breast cancer patients and others with illnesses have used writing as a therapeutic method to work their way through their emotions during times of uncertainty.

Writing and expressing your emotions, wishes, dreams, or disappointments on paper may help you develop a clear sense of direction and clarity. As you write about your loss and how you are dealing with it you can examine your thoughts, choices, and future plans. Individuals who have kept journals have noted that this healing activity has proved to be an essential step in their grief recovery.

One student was grateful that she had maintained a grief journal that she used to chronicle her progress. She added cut out pictures and poems that reminded her of her loved one. She now keeps this journal on her nightstand; it is a treasured keepsake filled with stories and memories of their time together.

Each person's crossing through grief is unique and every individual's experience and story is worth writing and saving. These precious memories can be documented in your journal. Embrace the opportunity to create your own personalized memory book by using *Write from Your Heart*.

Personal Writing

Write from Your Heart is a guided grief journal that encourages you to respond to the prompt at the head of each page. A prompt is a word or group of words meant to inspire you in your daily lesson. **The daily prompts have been constructed with care—each one serves a purpose to encourage you to think, meditate, motivate, write and heal.**

Healing Reflections

Group Journaling

Although this book may be used as a personal grief diary, it may also be used in a group setting.

Writing is therapeutic, relaxing, thought provoking and can help you sort out your ideas and emotions on paper. Keeping a journal allows you to create a personal keepsake that reflects your inner thoughts.

Individuals over the years have discovered that journal writing singly or as part of a group open up a new perspective on the grief experience.

Group writing can be a powerful and uplifting experience. One of the benefits of class participation is being able to share what others have written and to receive positive feedback on your own work.

While no two individuals experience grief in the same way, there is a commonality in the experience of grief, which in itself creates a bond between group members.

Grief writing isn't just about writing what has happened in your life, it is stepping beyond that point to a new plane, a place where you come to a conclusion of acceptance and peace. This journal is not meant to be a sourcebook of counseling, but a tool to use to work your way through grief — a personal grief diary.

Create a Tribute

Write from Your Heart will help you create a tribute to your loved one and also help you work through your feelings. These individuals who have so lovingly touched and influenced our lives will never be forgotten because they are woven into the very fabric of our existence.

We are the unique beings that we are today because of the love these people gave to us. You will carry this special love with you always as you learn to live with your grief.

In the future you will be able to pull this book out and thumb through it as you would a favorite photo album. Although it may be painful to write in your journal, it will eventually become a special keepsake of memories and of your honest emotions and thoughts.

And although it may seem impossible now, there will come a day when you will smile again. There will come a time when you will remember your loved one with joy instead of tears.

And even though our hearts are broken because these precious people were taken from us too soon, we can rejoice that we had the privilege of knowing and loving them, however brief the time.

Cherish those memories and share them in your journal pages.

Use this journal to express your feelings through the words that you pen. Each entry will add to the special memorial you are creating for your loved one. Remember to add drawings, pictures, or magazine cutouts, favorite sayings and items that will help make your book unique.

May you find comfort and peace as you write from the heart.

Week One

Begin to Heal

The following are a few of the prompts, verses and healing activities taken from *Write from Your Heart.*

Day One Prompt:

Dedicate this journal to the memory of a loved one.
Name and describe this person and your relationship.

Verse: *He heals the brokenhearted, and binds up their wounds. Psalms 147:3*

Day Two Healing Activity:

Take your journal outside and write about what you see. What is there that catches your eye? What do you hear or smell? Describe how you are feeling today.

When you are finished writing, look around and choose something in nature to take back with you — a leaf if you noticed the leaves or heard them rustling in the wind. Choose whatever you like: a feather, a flower, a little stone, a stick, or even a blade of grass.

This assignment is to help you focus on the beauty that is still all around you. Use your senses of sight, smell, hearing and touch to enjoy what God has created. Sometimes doing the ordinary can be extraordinary. See what you can discover, and write about it.

Verse:
May the God of hope fill you with all joy and peace as you trust in him, so that you may overflow with hope by the power of the Holy Spirit. Romans: 15:13

Day Three Prompt:

What gives you comfort?

Verse: *Blessed are those who mourn, for they will be comforted. Matthew 5:4.*

Day Four Prompt:

What are you afraid of or worry about? Does this verse give you comfort? Why?

Verse: *So do not fear, for I am with you; do not be dismayed, for I am your God. I will strengthen you and help you; I will uphold you with my righteous right hand. Isaiah 41: 10*

Day 5 Healing Activity.

Call someone whom you enjoy talking with—someone who encourages you. Write about why you enjoy knowing this person.

Quotes: *Find solace in friends and family, find peace in the word of God. Elaine Frissell*

Cry when you need to cry, rest when you are weary and reminisce when the need arises. For the tears are cleansing, the rest refreshing and the memories healing.
Kathrine Peterson

Permissions and Acknowledgments

The Other Side by Vernon C. Grounds, *Our Daily Bread*, Copyright 1994 by RBC Ministries, Grand Rapids, MI. Reprinted by permission

Nevertheless We Must Run Aground, From *Keep a Quiet Heart* by Elisabeth Elliot. ©1995 by Elisabeth Elliot. Published by Servant Publications, Box 8617, Ann Arbor, Michigan, 48107. Used with permission.

Jump Into Jesus' Arms from *Time to Get Serious* by Tony Evans, copyright © 1995, page 232. Used by permission of Crossway Books, a division of Good News Publishers, Wheaton, Illinois 60187.
p. 232

His Still Small Voice, *From Faith to Faith* by Kenneth and Gloria Copeland

Dr. Jane Robertson Westerfield, Baton Rouge, Louisiana.

The Miracle of the Vigil, The Assurance of Immortality, and *He is Alive*, Printed by Permission

How I Survived Grief and quotes by Fannie Palmer printed by permission

Dealing with Grief, printed by permission. Diane Crandall

The Day of the Dog Show Brownie Disappeared, Trasher's Lucky Day, and quotes by Elaine Frissell. Printed by permission

I Have Survived. By Shirley Caviness. Printed by permission.

Alexis, my dog, is a joy and true gift from God Karen Alexander, printed by permission.

The Mourning Doves of Peace by Linda Alexander, printed by permission

The Day the Clock Stopped by Helen Peterson, printed by permission.

Grampa Read me a Story by Bradley Palmer, printed by permission.

My son taught me that attitude is everything by Lisa Sitko, printed by permission

God sends us all kinds of signs of His mighty love by Doris Duplantis, printed by permission

Prayers by Pastor Stan Rockafellow, Fannie Palmer, Gail Sicard, Willie Pearl Scott, Diane Crandall, Donna Perkins, and Don Staples printed by permission.

Dove Lewis Pet assisted therapy program and *The Bond* by Geraldine and Curt Von Ahn, printed by permission

Jane Burfield,

Joseph Scriven (1819-1886) Hymn, What a friend we have in Jesus.